FIVE BAGS OF GOLD

A MODERN PARABLE OF WEALTH, RESPONSIBILITY, AND ETERNAL INVESTMENT

Nicholas Comninellis, MD

FIVE BAGS OF GOLD

A MODERN PARABLE OF WEALTH, RESPONSIBILITY, AND ETERNAL INVESTMENT

Nicholas Comninellis, MD
Founder of *INMED,*
the Institute for International Medicine

First printing: July 2025

New Leaf Press, P.O. Box 726, Green Forest, AR 72638

New Leaf Press is a division of the New Leaf Publishing Group, LLC.

ISBN: 978-0-89221-772-4
ISBN: 978-1-61458-941-9 (digital)
Library of Congress Control Number: 2025939621

Interior and Cover Design by Diana Bogardus

Please consider requesting that a copy of this volume be purchased by your local library system.

Printed in the United States of America

Visit our website for other great titles:
www.masterbooks.com

For information regarding promotional opportunities, contact the publicity department at pr@nlpg.com.

As a follower of Christ, how will you faithfully bless others with the talents and resources God has entrusted to you? Dr. Nicholas has masterfully highlighted our Biblically-based calling to care for those most in need. Ultimately, we will all give account of whether we elected (or not) to respond to this God-given directive. Through personal testimony and scripture, *Five Bags of Gold* profoundly motivates the reader to reflect on one's life and compels us to selflessly serve the forlorn and forgotten.

- **Lance Plyler, MD**
  Chief Medical Officer, Samaritan's Purse

I found this book to be well written, a very easy read, and also very thought-provoking. Given the unprecedented political, social, and economic turmoil of the day, *Five Bags of Gold* is not only timely but a much-needed reminder of how one should live. Why it is important to be of service to others over self, to treat others as we wish to be treated, and why there is a need to prioritize time for faith. The author continues to motivate and excite others to engage in humanitarian work. The growth of INMED is a shining example of the power of mentorship. The questions asked in the final portion of the book are wonderful opportunities for the reader to apply many of the lessons discussed throughout the book to their lives and proceed to identify how they too can be of service.

- **Tracy Branch**
  Captain, U.S. Public Health Service

This book is a powerful testament to lives lived—and still being lived—in humble obedience to Christ's call to serve "the least of these..." Matthew 25:40. With unwavering love, profound compassion, and relentless dedication, Dr. Nicholas brings the Gospel to life—not through words alone, but through selfless action. His journey and the journeys of others across nations, reaching the sick and vulnerable, reflects the true heart of a servant of God. Every page radiates a spiritual richness that reminds us that our greatest treasure lies not in what we keep, but in what we give. Dr. Nicholas's book also inspires me to develop and live by Treasure Investment Plan rooted in this principle.

- **Dr. Lawand Aqrawy**
  Associate Protection Officer at UNHCR, the UN Refugee Agency
  Law Professor at Akre University for Applied Sciences, Kurdistan Region of Iraq

Preface

Treasure — wealth, power, influence. We all want it. The desire is saturated throughout human nature and human history. But our use of treasure is controversial and provokes ceaseless creativity, corruption, generosity, and greed. *Five Bags of Gold: A Modern Parable Of Wealth, Responsibility, and Eternal Investment* explores virtue-guided use of our resources, illuminated by the author's personal experience on multiple continents with individuals investing their own bags of gold.

Part One:

What Do You Treasure?

For where your treasure is, there your heart will be also (Matthew 6:21).

Chapter 1
Treasure Received

Guo Li stepped carefully upon the bamboo scaffolding. Encased within stood an ancient Chinese pagoda. With reverence, Guo Li reached inward, scraping away the decaying paint that graced the revered monument to his culture and religious heritage. Pausing momentarily, Guo Li gazed out over the vast city, one hundred feet below. None of Shanghai's 25 million people would notice him — none but his fellow craftsmen working alongside.

Moving up one rung, Guo Li took a step, forced his weight on the next bamboo brace, and extended his leg. With a loud snap, the wood broke, sending Guo Li headfirst toward the street below. Guo Li let out a shout of terror and his colleagues gasped as they watched their friend dive toward death. Two seconds later, another crashing sound. The craftsmen peered over the scaffolding expecting to see their friend's crumpled body on the pavement. Instead, he was jackknifed over a beam below, his hands and feet dangling from where his abdomen was stopped by the bamboo.

They scurried downward, to Guo Li's heart-wrenching cries of pain. Forcing open a hatch on the pagoda's side, the craftsmen heaved his body inside and carried him down the winding circular staircase to the street below. Hurrying to the curb with their injured companion, the craftsmen waved for attention and shouted for motorists to stop. But Shanghai traffic is dense and intense, and deference is seldom rewarded. Minutes passed. No bus, truck, or even car driver seemed to notice their plight.

None, except a lowly elderly bicycle driver. His was a working bike designed to carry produce with a typical steerable front wheel, and two rear wheels supporting a wood-covered platform measuring about 4 x 6 feet. Guo Li, wincing with every movement, was laid on the platform. The elderly cyclist heaved his full weight on the front pedal. With the craftsmen trotting behind, the bike entered traffic and steered toward the distant horizon.

On that horizon I stood in the emergency department of Shanghai Charity Hospital where I served as a resident physician. The entryway consisted of a small brick arch just wide enough for a small car, and with an incline up to the entry doors. I heard shouting outside and emerged to see an exhausted old man straining against the petals of the three-wheeled bike and four men in work clothes pushing the bike from the rear. On the platform, a distressing sight: a crumpled young man clutching his abdomen and covered with bloody vomitus.

The emergency department attendants and I rushed him inside, the four men frantically describing the accident. Clearly, Guo Li suffered serious abdominal trauma, likely with rupture of his spleen, liver, and/or stomach. His blood pressure was low, and his heart rate was high, both indicating severe blood loss from internal bleeding. Guo Li would need emergency surgery. But my first priority was to stabilize his condition with intravenous fluid and blood replacement. The former was easy. Start an IV and administer medical-grade salt water. The latter proved more challenging than I anticipated.

"I need all of you to go to the laboratory and be tested to donate blood." I spoke to a rapidly growing group of Guo Li's colleagues, friends, and family members who were gathering in the waiting room. "Guo Li needs a blood transfusion immediately to save his life. Among you there surely are two or three who have the right blood type." I turned and started walking toward the lab, expecting all to follow. But I heard no steps behind me. I returned to the waiting room, where everyone sat still.

"如果不输血，国力就会死。但你可以帮助拯救他." I repeated. "Guo Li will die if he doesn't get a blood transfusion. But you can help save him." They looked at one another anxiously, and then their excuses began.

"I don't like needles."

"Sounds painful."

"I think I need all of my own blood."

"If I give away my blood, I will be giving away my soul."

"I really need to go home right now."

Exasperated, I tried my best to control my frustration at their self-centeredness, and appealed to their concern for Guo Li, a concern that just minutes earlier compelled them to come to the hospital. One by one, his family, friends, and coworkers stood up to leave.

In the background, Guo Li's cries of agony continued. An emergency department attendant came to the door. "Dr. Nicholas, we need you."

Nicholas Comninellis at the emergency entrance of Shanghai Charity Hospital. China, 1981. Credit: Author's photo.

TREASURE PARADOX

In His celebrated Sermon on the Mount, Christ Jesus declares: For where your treasure is, there your heart will be also (Matthew 6:21). What treasure is He speaking about? Treasure can refer to something material like money, property, or possessions — for example, the gifts of gold, frankincense, and myrrh brought by the Magi to the Christ child in Bethlehem. Treasure may also refer to spiritual wealth, including wisdom, love, spiritual understanding, and the Good News. In short, treasure in the biblical sense means a thing of great value.

What we treasure bears witness to our values, our priorities, and our faith. What we dwell upon in our discretionary moments, where our mind goes when undistracted, what we do with uncommitted resources, all reveal what is most important to us. As Saint Augustine observed, "You are what you love," and what we love guides our actions.

When we first consider treasure, images and sentiments of hard work, diligent study, and relentless toil often come to mind. The great paradox of treasure, however, is that the most significant treasure is one we cannot earn or create, but rather one that we actively receive. In his moment of crisis, by comparison, Guo Li could not possibly acquire blood on his own behalf. Rather, he needed to receive it. Description of this special treasure is seeded throughout the New Testament and can be summed up with the mnemonic **L I F E**:

CHRIST'S **L**OVE

Each of us has a deep, built-in need for belonging, for love. We need to feel appreciated and respected by someone we admire. Our parents and friends may try to fill this need. However, most love is conditional upon our performance, meaning we will be loved if we measure up, appear attractive, or perform well.

But the love of Christ is quite different. He loves us just as we are and not as we should be. His is a love without preconditions; a love that we can't earn. Paul, one of the first followers of Jesus, put it like this: "...he saved us, not because of righteous things we had done, but because of his mercy... through Jesus Christ our Savior" (Titus 3:5-6). With the absolute assurance of God's love, we can find energy, hope, and even enthusiasm for living.

CHRIST'S INSPIRATION

Everyone needs a sense of capability, a feeling of confidence to better handle life's demands. But such a sentiment alone is fragile and subject to the whims of emotional swings.

When we trust in Christ, we benefit from more than just a confident feeling. We receive the Holy Spirit (1 Corinthians 3:16–17, Ephesians 1:13–14). Part of God Himself comes to live within us, infusing the abilities and energy we need to overcome life's obstacles. Paul explains: "For the Spirit God gave us does not make us timid, but gives us power, love and self-discipline" (2 Timothy 1:7). Christ's inspiration is not just an emotion. It's a reality — the person of God active within us, and this is inspiration in the most potent sense.

CHRIST'S FORGIVENESS

Offense against God, others, and even against ourselves is a tragic fact; one usually followed by feelings of guilt and shame. It also generates real world problems: war, starvation, disabilities, disease, and relationship turmoil of all kinds. We can try to overcome the offense through denial, distraction, or self-sacrifice. But the offense — the sin — remains a burden people carry throughout their lives. Why? Because sin is a spiritual problem. No amount of self-improvement can detach it. Only Christ can lift it off from us.

When we trust Christ to forgive us, remarkable changes occur. Spiritually, we are freed from absolutely all guilt before God. Mentally, we gain the strongest possible rationale to combat shame. Socially, we receive the foundation to rebuild our relationships. In Paul's letter to the church at Colossae he describes the depth of Jesus' forgiveness: "When you were dead in your sins and in the uncircumcision of your flesh, God made you alive with Christ. He forgave us all our sins, having canceled the charge of our legal indebtedness, which stood against us and condemned us; he has taken it away, nailing it to the cross" (Colossians 2:13–14). Our account with God is completely and permanently cleared!

CHRIST'S ETERNITY

It's natural to want to preserve our own lives. In our teens and twenties, this seems easy. But in our thirties and beyond, a sobering reality sets in — the fact that life will not last forever. Relatives and friends begin to die, education and career dreams become unachievable, our hair grays, our skin wrinkles. In this light, Ecclesiastes uses metaphors like dust, smoke, and shadow to describe the brevity of human existence. For people with no anticipation of life after death, depression and hopelessness become common, and even understandable.

But the expectation is much different for individuals who trust Christ. Though our bodies decline, we hold onto a wonderful promise. In 1 Peter 1:3–4, we read, "Praise be to the God and Father of our Lord Jesus Christ! In his great mercy he has given us new birth into a living hope through the resurrection of Jesus Christ from the dead, and into an inheritance that can never perish, spoil or fade. This inheritance is kept in heaven for you." No matter what tragedy we encounter on Earth, God promises us an incredible life forever in heaven. Holding on to this truth can give us remarkable courage amid this life's challenges. The reality is that eternal life begins not when we die, but the very moment we begin to trust in Christ.

Our individual pursuit of treasure is better navigated by first recognizing that the most significant treasure cannot be earned or created. Rather, the **LIFE** — Love, Inspiration, Forgiveness, and Eternity in Christ — is available to us through His sacrifice on our behalf.

TREASURE WITHIN

Guo Li clutched his abdomen, which continued to grow slightly in size, no doubt due to the bleeding within. I administered morphine to control his pain and pressed on the bags of intravenous fluid to speed the flow infusing into his veins to help maintain blood pressure. But the effort was losing effectiveness. Guo Li's blood pressure, temporarily sustained, began falling once again. For a moment, I considered offering my own blood. But an episode of hepatitis years earlier made my blood unsafe for donation.

I hustled back to the waiting room. The family was gone. The friends and coworkers had also disappeared. One middle-aged man remained. His face was wrinkled, signaling years of unrelenting outdoor labor. His clothing, covered with fine coal dust, suggested humble housing without laundry. He spoke with a heavy accent common among village people who migrated to Shanghai to fill the lowest paid manual jobs.

The man signaled with his hand.

"You still need blood, I believe. I'll give my blood!"

"Who are you?" I replied, quite surprised.

"Well, I'm the bicycle driver." He spoke matter-of-factly.

Not a hint of pride or self-sacrifice tainted his voice.

As if anticipating my questions, he continued. "I think my body has an abundance of blood, and if my blood is my soul then surely my soul can help give a bit of life to another."

The two of us walked to the laboratory. Indeed, the driver was a blood type match, and within the time necessary to change a bicycle tire's inner tube, Guo Li was receiving his transfusion.

I spoke with the surgeon and anesthesiologist, who were delighted at the news, and rolled Guo Li toward the operating room. A couple of hours later, my patient was in recovery, fresh from the repair of his bleeding spleen. His family and coworkers also reappeared, expressing relief and acting a bit sheepish as they inquired about Guo Li's condition.

One person among them finally confessed what was surely on everyone's mind: "How fortunate that someone, even a total stranger, actually treasured him more than we did."

Nicholas Comninellis with resident physicians on night duty at Shanghai Charity Hospital. China, 1983. Credit: Author's photo.

Chapter 2

Treasure Desired

Long before my arrival in Shanghai, a London-trained physician, William Lockhart (October 3,1811 – April 29, 1896) rented a house in the Big East Gate neighborhood of Shanghai. He cared for those who were sick — often from tuberculosis, cholera, and malaria — and in 1844 opened the first Western-style hospital in Shanghai — only the second such hospital in all of China. This was the 24th year of the Qing Dynasty, the very last of China's imperial reigns. From its humble launch, Shanghai Charity Hospital, 仁济医院，grew quickly to 60 inpatient beds plus a bustling outpatient clinic.

In caring for his patients, Dr. Lockhart observed, "The feeling of confidence on the part of the patients is worthy of notice. One of these patients was reminded shortly before the operation (for a large tumor on his neck) that with all the care that could be taken, the result was sometimes fatal.

"He (the patient) interrupted the remark by saying, 'I have been too long acquainted with you, Doctor, have seen too much in this hospital with my own eyes, to require anything now to inspire my confidence.'

"The operation was successful, and the man, soon restored to health, returned to his family. His father, who was a learned man, wrote a letter of thanks for the kind treatment of his son, saying 'This certainly is a remarkable, difficult, and dangerous disease, at which other men fold their arms in despair; but the doctor, delighted and rejoiced at his ability for the task, seized the knife and cut, not causing many wounds: so that one may say, he is able to do what is of difficult performance to others —yea, can execute what is impossible for other men.'"

Dr. Lockhart describes his reaction to the letter of thanks: "When I commenced this paper my heart skipped like the sparrow from delight indescribable."[1]

Such moments of solace were uncommon. Working in this small facility, with few medications or supplies, and multitudes of people afflicted by disease and injury, staff at Shanghai Charity Hospital described their sense of crushing pressure. One colleague, Dr. Peter Parker, recounts, "Years of toil; and all the responsibility of one who has been entrusted with the health and lives of thousands, and tens of thousands of fellowmen, embracing every condition of life, from the beggar to the member of the imperial house; every grade of office from the street-constable to the imperial commissioner. Wearisome days and sleepless nights have been spent; the best of my days have been devoted to the labor of endeavoring, with the divine blessing, to arrest maladies that were hastening their victims to the grave."[2]

The future of the hospital was in peril. Where would relief come for those like Dr. Parker?

Dr. Peter Parker. 1840s painting by Lam Qua. Credit: Public Domain. File:Dr. Peter Parker.jpg, Wikimedia Commons, Accessed March 2, 2025. https://commons.wikimedia.org/wiki/Category:Peter_Parker_(physician)#/media/File:Dr._Peter_Parker.jpg

---

1 Lockhart, William. *The Medical Missionary in China: a narrative of 20 year's experience*. Second Edition. London: Hurst And Blackett, Publishers. 1861. P 163.

2 Lockhart, William. *The Medical Missionary in China: a narrative of 20 year's experience*. Second Edition. London: Hurst And Blackett, Publishers. 1861. P 175.

~TREASURE DESIRED

What do you currently treasure? What do you dwell upon in your discretionary moments? Where does your mind go when it is undistracted? What do you do with your uncommitted resources?

Chances are very high that your current treasures are among the five P's.

POSSESSIONS

The allure of possessions is indeed universal. At that time in Shanghai, most people survived on the equivalent of $10 USD per month. Homes were not heated and running water sometimes only available at public dispensaries. My closest friends pined for a single-speed bicycle, a cassette tape player, or a simple camera of their own.

We all need possessions. But there is enormous pressure to overemphasize their importance. Many people around the world believe they do not amount to much until they own a respectable house, new-model cars, and a handsome wardrobe.

By contract, Christ emphasizes a contradictory perspective on possessions:

> "... life does not consist in an abundance of possessions."
> "...The ground of a certain rich man yielded an abundant harvest. He thought to himself, 'What shall I do? I have no place to store my crops.'
>
> "Then he said, 'This is what I'll do. I will tear down my barns and build bigger ones, and there I will store my surplus grain. And I'll say to myself, "You have plenty of grain laid up for many years. Take life easy; eat, drink and be merry."'
> "But God said to him, 'You fool! This very night your life will be demanded from you. Then who will get what you have prepared for yourself?'
>
> "This is how it will be with whoever stores up things for themselves but is not rich toward God."

Some possessions are essential to life. But we are deluded when we define our treasure solely by what we own.

POSITION

The allure of position is global as well. The strong desire among some to be president, governor, principal, founder, chief, manager, or foreman is unrelenting.

Is gaining a position a sufficient treasure? King Herod during the time of Christ held absolute authority over the people of Israel. He answered only to the emperor of the Roman Empire. Defending his powerful position was essential to Herod. In Matthew chapter 2, we read that foreign ambassadors, the Magi, came to honor the Christ child. They went to Herod and asked, "Where is the one who is born king of the Jews?"

Herod became incensed. He was the king of the Jews! Who was this baby forecast to replace him? Herod wanted to find that child, and when the Magi didn't help, Herod sent his soldiers to kill all the young boys in the town where the Christ was born. Ensuring that his position was unchallenged, in Herod's mind, was even worth the cost of these innocent lives.

Some 30 years later, Paul of Tarsus was one of Israel's most powerful religious leaders, and the one appointed to prosecute and suppress the first Christ-followers. Nevertheless, Paul abandoned his position when he discovered what was more important, declaring, "But whatever were gains to me I now consider loss for the sake of Christ. What is more, I consider everything a loss compared to the surpassing worth of knowing Christ Jesus my Lord, for whose sake I have lost all things. I consider them garbage, that I may gain Christ" (Philippians 3:7–8).

We certainly need talented leaders in positions of authority. Without them, our schools, governments, and businesses would quickly fail. Yet, holding a position only for position's sake is empty at the least, and may even become a precursor of evil. In establishing the Mongol Empire, for example, Genghis Khan (a.d. 1162–1227) succeeded in ruling Europe and Asia, spanning from the Atlantic Ocean in the west all the way to the Pacific Ocean in the east. In doing so, he also became responsible for slaughtering 40 to 60 million people — 2-5% of the entire world population.

PLEASURE

Pleasure is another great treasure. Everyone enjoys some form of sports, arts, music, travel, or theater. Engaging in personal pleasures plays a crucial role in overall well-being. Whether it's reading a book, listening to music, enjoying a favorite meal, or pursuing a hobby — these seemingly small yet meaningful experiences can significantly enhance mental, emotional, and even physical health. Stress relief often results, and thereby reduces anxiety and tension, boosts motivation and creativity, sparks sentiments of joy, and fosters richer relationships.

Yet, unbridled pleasure can have a dark side. King Solomon, the successor of the patriarch David and builder of the first temple in Jerusalem, placed a high priority on romantic pleasure.

> King Solomon, however, loved many foreign women besides Pharaoh's daughter — Moabites, Ammonites, Edomites, Sidonians and Hittites. They were from nations about which the LORD had told the Israelites, "You must not intermarry with them, because they will surely turn your hearts after their gods." Nevertheless, Solomon held fast to them in love. He had seven hundred wives of royal birth and three hundred concubines, and his wives led him astray. As Solomon grew old, his wives turned his heart after other gods, and his heart was not fully devoted to the LORD his God, as the heart of David his father had been. He followed Ashtoreth the goddess of the Sidonians, and Molek the detestable god of the Ammonites. So, Solomon did evil in the eyes of the LORD; he did not follow the LORD completely, as David his father had done (1 Kings 11:1–6).

As a rebuke against Solomon's womanizing and unfaithfulness, biblical Scripture records how God raised up multiple adversaries against him, including neighboring nations, those among his own officials, and even Solomon's own family members. Life would be difficult and monotonous without periods of relaxation and recreation. But the sole pursuit of pleasure as treasure is a perilous one.

PROJECTS

Some people allocate great value to projects, campaigns, or enterprises. They dedicate themselves to building companies, perfecting hobbies, securing athletic achievements, or composing books. Project-oriented people experience deep satisfaction from advancing and completing such undertakings.

Is it worthwhile to build our lives around such work? King Herod undertook a massive project: reconstruction of the ancient temple of Israel. It became one of the largest buildings in the Roman Empire, twice as large as Rome's largest temple, and capable of accommodating hundreds of thousands of pilgrims at once.

A marvel of engineering, this marble and gold structure 46 years in the making was intended by Herod "to assure his eternal remembrance."[3] (*Antiquities* 15.380). Yet in Matthew 24:1-2, we read Christ's assessment of its significance:

> "Jesus left the temple and was walking away when his disciples came up to him to call his attention to its buildings. 'Do you see all these things?' he asked. 'Truly I tell you, not one stone here will be left on another; every one will be thrown down.'"

This great building — one erected ostensibly for the worship of God — didn't impress Christ at all. He was focused on a treasure of a different kind. We, too, can give ourselves to many great undertakings: building a business, producing a work of art, creating a political movement, or making a scientific discovery. But Christ is not primarily interested in our projects.

FOUR-FOLD TREASURES

Consider one man who had everything: possessions, position, pleasure, and projects. King Solomon of Israel was reported by historians to be the richest, wisest, and most powerful man of his time. Yet, what did he think of himself? Solomon is credited with writing in Ecclesiastes 2:3-11:

> … I wanted to see what was good for people to do under the heavens during the few days of their lives. I undertook great projects: I built houses for myself and planted vineyards. I made gardens and parks and planted all kinds of fruit trees in them. I made reservoirs to water groves of flourishing trees. I bought male and female slaves and had other slaves

3 Flavius Josephus, *Antiquities of the Jews* 15.380

> who were born in my house. I also owned more herds and flocks than anyone in Jerusalem before me. I amassed silver and gold for myself, and the treasure of kings and provinces. I acquired male and female singers, and a harem as well—the delights of a man's heart. I became greater by far than anyone in Jerusalem before me. In all this my wisdom stayed with me. I denied myself nothing my eyes desired; I refused my heart no pleasure. My heart took delight in all my labor, and this was the reward for all my toil. Yet when I surveyed all that my hands had done and what I had toiled to achieve, everything was meaningless, a chasing after the wind; nothing was gained under the sun.

Consider also the opinion of famed National Football League quarterback Tom Brady, winner of seven Super Bowls and the NFL's all-time leader in passing yards. In 2005, Tom Brady appeared on 60 Minutes:

> "I have three Super Bowl rings, and still I think there's got to be something greater out there. This can't be what it's all cracked up to be," observed Brady.
>
> "What's the answer?" asked correspondent Steve Kroft.
>
> "I wish I knew," Brady said. "I wish I knew."[4]

Focus on the statements of Brady and Solomon. These men who "had it all" still were not satisfied. Many of us today are not satisfied, either. Like them, we pursue possessions, position, pleasure, and projects, and still feel emptiness deep inside. We have amassed material riches, attained high acclaim, checked off our bucket list, and succeeded where others have failed. Yet we still sense futility. What is missing?

PEOPLE

Once Christ was addressing a crowd of people, when someone posed a question about priorities:

> One of them, an expert in the law, tested him with this question: "Teacher, which is the greatest commandment in

4 "The Super Bowl Is Not Enough." H.E. Butt Foundation. From Tom Brady Talks to Steve Kroft, *60 Minutes*. Nov. 6, 2005. https://hebfdn.org/portfolio/the-super-bowl-is-not-enough/, accessed March 3, 2025.

> the Law?" Jesus replied, "'Love the Lord your God with all your heart and with all your soul and with all your mind.' This is the first and greatest commandment. And the second is like it: 'Love your neighbor as yourself.' All the Law and the Prophets hang on these two commandments" (Matthew 22:35–40).

What is the treasure Christ values? God and people. His proclamation was challenging to those of that time. They, like we do today, treasure other things, the other four P's (possessions, position, projects, pleasure). But to Christ, how we value God and other people is the best measure of our wealth.

WHAT IS THIS LOVE?

When Christ admonishes us to love God and love our neighbors, what kind of love does He speak? This single word has multiple meanings in the English language, as eloquently described by C.S. Lewis in *The Four Loves*:[5]

- A powerful affection for another person, such as one's love for their friends or family members
- A strong enjoyment of or interest in something, such as one's love of music or history
- An intense fondness for a person of the opposite sex

When Christ speaks of loving God and others, He is not referring to the closeness shared between friends, the attraction of an object or pastimes, nor the sensual love felt between couples. Rather, Christ is speaking of a unique kind of love — agape love. Agape is a commitment love, a love that sacrifices for the welfare of another, despite the personal costs. First Corinthians 13:4–7 gives us a clear picture of agape. It can be paraphrased like this:

> People with love in their hearts are patient and kind toward others, never acting jealous, boastful, or arrogantly. They do not behave poorly or selfishly, and do not hold grudges. People who truly love never wish evil upon anyone, but instead always work for the well-being of others.

Christ sacrificed Himself for our welfare and calls us to embrace the power of agape love as we do the same for those in our world.

---

5 C.S. Lewis. *The Four Loves* (Boston, MA: Mariner Books, 1971).

TREASURE DESIRED

Consider the options again. We can work to win an exalted position, gain exquisite possessions, complete fantastic projects, experience marvelous pleasures, and/or invest in the value of people. Actually, most individuals work toward some combination of treasures, such as:

- Becoming president of the company (position)
- Acquiring a fine house and car (possessions)
- Finishing a college degree (projects)
- Vacationing in the mountains (pleasure)
- Building excellent relationships (people)

Is there anything wrong with these? Not necessarily. We depend upon skilled leaders in key positions. We need certain possessions to ease life's workload. There are many virtuous projects. And we all need to relax and have fun. The prevailing deficiency, however, is the low priority given to people. People, while the most important, must compete against stronger position-conscious, possession-oriented, project-focused, and pleasure-seeking interests.

Here is a profound truth: We can treasure people by utilizing our position, possessions, projects, and even our pleasures for their benefit.

My mentors at Shanghai Charity Hospital were physicians in their 60s and 70s. Most received their education in the 1940s and 50s at Saint John's University Medical School in Shanghai, staffed by faculty from the University of Pennsylvania. Unsurprisingly, my mentor's English language was perfect.

But not so among younger physicians, who pursued me to help them improve their fluency. I initially felt quite ambivalent. I was striving to improve my own Mandarin speaking skills, and investing more time speaking English seemed counterproductive. Yet I also came to realize that one very tangible way to demonstrate how I value my colleagues would be to help them communicate using the most useful language in today's world.

So, in the evenings these young people came to my dorm room, and we read together, focusing on pronunciation and vocabulary. Afternoons in the hospital classroom, I guided them through group conversation on health-related subjects. Occasionally a baffling grammar question was posed, to which I would confess I did not know the answer. Nevertheless, their gratefulness was evident through comments like, "You us very we appreciate," reinforcing to me the importance of continuing to offer them ample learning opportunities.

Nicholas Comninellis in the prevailing attire of the day, the Chairman Mao suit. Shanghai, China, 1981. Credit: Author's Photo.

REVERENCE FOR LIFE

While living in Shanghai, I became inspired by another physician quite similar to William Lockhart and Peter Parker. Albert Schweitzer (1875–1965), born in Alsace — bordering France and Germany — was a gifted scholar, and by age 30 had earned doctorates in theology and philosophy. Schweitzer also transposed Bach's renowned orchestra compositions to organ, and he traveled throughout Europe with the Paris Bach Society performing this organ music to considerable acclaim.

But in 1905, while still age 30, Schweitzer read an appeal from the Paris Missionary Society for a physician to serve in west Africa. One biographer documents what happened next: "Amid a hail of protests from his friends, family, and colleagues, Schweitzer resigned his post and re-entered the university as a student in a three-year course toward the degree of Doctorate in Medicine.... He planned to spread the Gospel by the example of his Christian labor of healing...."[6]

6 "Albert Schweitzer." Wikipedia. https://en.wikipedia.org/wiki/Albert_Schweitzer. Ac-

Over the next 50 years — including a period being imprisoned during World War I — Albert Schweitzer lived in what became of the nation of Gabon, West Africa. His biographies are filled with compassionate accounts of caring for Africans who suffered from dysentery, malaria, sleeping sickness, leprosy, poisonings, and surgical emergencies. He also regularly entertained visitors to the hospital through organ recitals well into the nights. Throughout those decades, Dr. Schweitzer also continued to compose works of theology and philosophy, most notably *The Quest of the Historical Jesus* (a rebuttal against growing liberal interpretation of Scripture) and literary works expanding the principle of *Reverence for Life* — appreciation for the image of God within each person. Albert Schweitzer, still working in obscurity, was recognized with the Nobel Peace Prize in 1953 for his humanitarian work and for modeling the sanctity of humankind.

Reverence for life. It is another way of describing people prioritized. Albert Sweitzer. He is another example for those of us following Christ today of long-serving, humble, self-sacrifice to make people prioritized.

Albert Schweitzer — Dutch National Archives, The Hague, Fotocollectie Algemeen Nederlands Persbureau (ANEFO), 1945-1989 bekijk toegang 2.24.01.04 Bestanddeeln

---

cessed March 8, 2025.

SHANGHAI PEOPLE PRIORITIZED

By the early 1900s, Shanghai Charity Hospital's obstacles seemed insurmountable: crumbling buildings and infrastructure, repeated typhoid outbreaks driving throngs of patients seeking care, and precious little access to the rapidly growing advances in medicine abroad.

Into this gap stepped Henry Lester (1840–1926), one whose achievements in life could not have been anticipated. Lester was born in Southampton in 1840, where all his brothers died from an unknown disease. In sadness and dissolution, Lester booked passage on a cargo ship to China with no plans other than to start a new life. In Shanghai, he grew to become a wildly successful merchant and architect, responsible for constructing the city's most iconic buildings on the Bund — the waterfront area in historic central Shanghai.

A devout Christian Puritan, as Lester advanced in years, he saw an opportunity to put his resources into faith-motivated action. In 1927, Shanghai Charity Hospital received from Lester a gift of 81,000 pounds of silver and four lots of real estate. These were used to enlarge the hospital and modernize the medical technology. By 1932, a new six story hospital — the very building where I worked — had been constructed and the number of beds increased from 60 to 250.

How did Henry Lester treasure people? By directing his position, possessions, and projects toward meeting the compelling humanitarian needs of Shanghai's citizens. As observed by Dr. Parker, "To the deaf, hearing; to the blind, sight; to the dying, life, have been instrumentally restored. I have had the gratification of seeing some who have survived severe operations for five, ten, and even twenty years, who had diseases which would have long since terminated in death if they had not been arrested" (treated).[7]

Bringing to a close my two years at Shanghai Charity Hospital in 1983, I would assure Dr. William Lockhart, the founder, Henry Lester, the funder, and Dr. Peter Parker, the long-serving humble professional, that the good work they began 140 years earlier was continuing with vigor.

---

7 Lockhart, William. *The Medical Missionary in China: a narrative of 20 year's experience.* Second Edition. London: Hurst And Blackett, Publishers. 1861. P 175.

Henry Lester, architect and philanthropist. Credit: AHRnet, Lester, Henry 1840 – 1926. https://architecture.arthistoryresearch.net/architects/lester-henry. Accessed March 2, 2025.

Part Two:

What Account Will You Give for Your Treasure?

"... I tell you the truth, whatever you did for one of the least of these brothers of mine, you did for me ...."
(Matthew 25:32–40)

Chapter 3

Treasure Report

In the 15th century, the Portuguese began to occupy the region of southwest Africa that today makes up the country of Angola. Their intention was the extraction of wealth — primarily cotton, sugar, ivory, timber, and slaves. In 1961, Angolan fighters began to resist the Portuguese, culminating in 1974 with national independence. But civil war immediately ensued between Angola's two major national political parties, fueled by weapons and soldiers from Cuba, South Africa, the Soviet Union, and the United States.

At the time of national independence, almost all healthcare facilities in Angola were sponsored by churches, including 120 hospitals by some counts. As combat escalated, almost all these facilities were abandoned or destroyed. Nevertheless, Angolan church leaders held fast to their deeply rooted desire to provide compassionate healthcare for their people — those suffering the devastating and preventable consequences of malaria, measles, malnutrition, and more.

In 1988 a request from Angolan churches was circulated in the United States for an American physician to come and assist them with this mission. The circumstances would be austere: physical danger, little financial support, and enormous human need.

JOHN THE BAPTIST

Early one morning, a simple farmer, John the Baptist by name, filled his well-worn burlap bag with corn seeds. He glanced around the one-room house, built years earlier from dried mud blocks. John the Baptist's wife and teenage sons were still sleeping as he quickly consumed a breakfast of boiled cornmeal. Though he could not afford sugar or milk, the familiar, gritty taste was satisfying.

John the Baptist stepped outdoors and strolled toward the hills in the distance. As the sunlight burned off the fog, he could appreciate the lush landscape. He passed a defunct military tank immobilized on a hillside. The wreck of a Russian MiG fighter aircraft lay derelict 100 meters away. But these hazards weighed very little upon his mind compared with what lay just beneath the earth. Land mines, ten to fifteen million, were salted throughout the countryside.

John the Baptist arrived at his field, one marked only by a familiar perimeter of trees and boulders. With a metal rod, he drove holes into the ground and added two or three grains of seed corn to each. This action was the last he remembered.

The day was growing longer and beginning to cast shadows on the tiny houses surrounding John the Baptist's home. His sons grew concerned. "Papa should have been home two hours ago! It's becoming cold, and in the darkness, Papa will have trouble finding his way." So, the two adolescents began trotting toward the field, some 2 km away, where they anticipated finding their father.

In the deepening darkness, the two boys made out the figure of a man lying face down in the cornfield. It was their papa! He lay motionless, covered with mud and blood next to a crooked hole in the ground. John the Baptist's left leg was missing. Frantically, the boys consider their options. The closest health facility was a two-day walk. Would their father survive?

Shouts erupted from the rotunda at Kalukembe Hospital — the nation's sole functioning church-sponsored medical center. I paused my evaluation of a febrile child to walk outside. Two young men were shouting, "Ajude-nos!" "Help us!" In their arms, front and rear, was a homemade stretcher crafted from tree limbs. Suspended between these were shreds of clothing supporting a gray-haired man. He lay motionless, one leg wrapped in a gunny sack.

We quickly moved to triage, where John the Baptist had no measurable blood pressure. When we unwrapped the leg, fragments of his bare tibial bone, stripped of muscle and skin, jutted out where the lower leg had been. John's foot was completely gone. The shredded muscles close to the knee draped over the upper leg in an ugly mass. The flesh smelled horribly, for the wound was now two days old. I turned my head away to fight off my nausea.

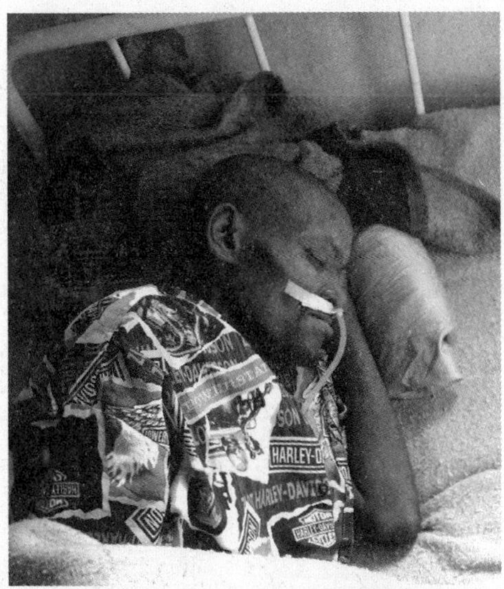

John the Baptist in recovery at Kalukembe Hospital following surgery for his landmine injury. Angola, 1989. Credit: Author's photo.

I suspected that this farmer might also have suffered brain damage from the blood loss, possibly even a stroke. The first priority was to replenish his blood from our modestly stocked laboratory, along with intravenous fluid. Then, we moved him to the operating room.

The nurse administering anesthesia urged, "Let's pray for him." Laying his hand on the head of John the Baptist, he proceeded. "Christ Jesus, we're shaken over the trauma suffered by this man. We know that You love him. Please help him recover and please help us now to do our part."

With a soapy sponge I scrubbed the leg and drew a line where I would amputate. Next, I wrapped the mangled lower leg in a sterile sheet to keep it from contaminating the amputation site and began the incision below his knee. As I worked, I kept an eye on the blood transfusion dripping into John the Baptist's vein. Blood was what he needed most, but it seemed to flow too slowly. After half an hour the amputation was finished, and we moved the man to intensive care.

There, John the Baptist continued to lie motionless, not even flinching when disturbed by an injection needle. After hours of life-saving work, it appeared to me that he would not survive. I departed, fully expecting that by morning his bed would be empty.

ACCOUNTABLE

Christ realized that soon He would be arrested and executed. Time was growing short to emphasize again to His disciples their mission to teach all people to obey everything Christ had taught them. In this context, Christ described the future ultimate judgment of humanity, often referred to as the Parable of the Sheep and the Goats:

> "When the Son of Man comes in his glory, and all the angels with him, he will sit on his glorious throne. All the nations will be gathered before him, and he will separate the people one from another as a shepherd separates the sheep from the goats. He will put the sheep on his right and the goats on his left.
>
> "Then the King will say to those on his right, 'Come, you who are blessed by my Father; take your inheritance, the kingdom prepared for you since the creation of the world. For I was hungry and you gave me something to eat, I was thirsty and you gave me something to drink, I was a stranger and you invited me in, I needed clothes and you clothed me, I was sick and you looked after me, I was in prison and you came to visit me.'
>
> "Then the righteous will answer him, 'Lord, when did we see you hungry and feed you, or thirsty and give you something to drink? When did we see you a stranger and invite you in, or needing clothes and clothe you? When did we see you sick or in prison and go to visit you?'
>
> "The King will reply, 'Truly I tell you, whatever you did for one of the least of these brothers and sisters of mine, you did for me.'
>
> "Then he will say to those on his left, 'Depart from me, you who are cursed, into the eternal fire prepared for the devil and his angels. For I was hungry and you gave me nothing to eat, I was thirsty and you gave me nothing to drink, I was a stranger and you did not invite me in, I needed clothes and you did not clothe me, I was sick and in prison and you did not look after me.'

> "They also will answer, 'Lord, when did we see you hungry or thirsty or a stranger or needing clothes or sick or in prison, and did not help you?'
>
> "He will reply, 'Truly I tell you, whatever you did not do for one of the least of these, you did not do for me.'
>
> "Then they will go away to eternal punishment, but the righteous to eternal life" (Matthew 25:31–46).

In Christ's parable, what is the treasure upon which ultimate judgment is based? What are the implications for how we shall live today?

This preview of our coming appearance before Christ contains powerful principles applicable for how we live today. First, the central criterion for His judgment of our lives is not the correctness of our belief system nor our adherence with religious ceremonies. Rather, Christ will consider our acts of compassion.

A profound corollary of such compassion is the presence of Christ in those who are needy. "Truly I tell you, whatever you did not do for one of the least of these, you did not do for me," reveals a deep spiritual truth: Christ identifies with those who are humble, poor, and marginalized. These words challenge us to see Christ in such people, reinforcing the biblical fact that true love for God is demonstrated through true love for others.

Most sobering of all is the eternal consequences of our actions described in this treatise. The final separation by Christ of the sheep and goats foresees the eternal destinies of these people: eternal life for the compassionate and eternal punishment for the heartless.

How we make use of the treasure placed in our hands is pivotal to our spiritual destiny. To say this is not to negate the Good News of Christ's sacrifice and gift of forgiveness offered to each person, but to emphasize that those who truly trust in Christ will obey Him by feeding those who are hungry, offering drink to those who are thirsty, sharing hospitality with strangers, clothing those who are cold, visiting those who are sick or in prison, and any number of other means demonstrating compassion and addressing the needs of humankind.

CONFLICTING PARADIGMS OF GREATNESS

The strongman image of greatness contrasts sharply with greatness as projected in Parable of the Sheep and the Goats. The strongman approach to greatness is built on power, dominance, and self-exaltation. It seeks to achieve superiority through force, control, and personal achievement, often by suppressing others. This mindset of the strongman values success by worldly standards — material wealth, influence, and status — defining strength as the ability to impose one's will and to command respect through fear or manipulation.

By contrast, greatness in the sight of Christ is marked by humility, servanthood, and self-sacrificial love. In this light, Christ redefined true greatness, saying, "… whoever wants to become great among you must be your servant" (Matthew 20:26). Instead of seeking strongman power, Christ declared that true greatness is found in humbling oneself, serving others, and embracing weakness as a model through which God's strength is revealed (2 Corinthians 12:9).

While the strongman seeks to exalt himself, Christ calls on His followers to deny themselves. His kingdom is an upside-down reality where those who are last shall be first, and the greatest are those who humble themselves before God and intentionally serve others with vigor.

PROFOUND WICKEDNESS

Of all the horrific actors over the last century, some rise to the top as the most diabolical. Consider these tragic examples.

Adolf Hitler began his adult life by studying art and even considering theology. But amid the turmoil following World War I, Hitler changed course and rose through the ranks of the German government, where, in 1933 he declared himself Führer — that is, supreme leader or dictator. Hitler's worldview was steeped in nationalism, racial superiority, and anti-Semitism. He surrounded himself with dedicated deputies who would do his bidding. In 1939, Hitler's armies invaded Poland, igniting World War II in Europe. Everywhere his deputies traveled they diligently searched for Jews, Gypsies, and disabled persons, all deemed unfit to live and destined for execution. In all, 15–20 million Europeans — roughly the population of the Netherlands — died as a result of Hitler's war.[1]

---

1 "The Blast of World War II", *Britannica.* https://www.britannica.com/topic/history-of-Europe/The-blast-of-World-War-II. Accessed March 4, 2025.

Timothy McVeigh was consumed with anti-government sentiment and deeply angered over his perception of federal authority overreach. The result was his horrific planned revenge. McVeigh created a truck bomb consisting of 5,000 pounds of fuel oil and ammonium nitrate. He drove up to the Alfred P. Murrah Federal Building entrance in Oklahoma City, selected for its symbol of government authority. In plain view of the entrance on the second floor was the building's childcare center. McVeigh put in his earplugs, lit the fuse, and nonchalantly walked away. Seconds later, the explosion killed 19 of those children, along with extinguishing the lives of 149 adults and injuring 600 more. In United States history, McVeigh's crime continues to be the deadliest domestic terrorist attack.

Bashar al-Assad became president of Syria in 2000. This nation in the Middle East — surrounded by Turkey, Iraq, Jordan, Israel, and Lebanon — was at that time already one of the poorest in the world. Bashar al-Assad initially appeared to be an unlikely ruler. Working as an ophthalmologist in the United Kingdom, he helped restore sight to people with visual impairment. But upon inheriting his family dynasty, Bashar al-Assad's vision changed to hardening his rule through a crackdown on dissent. Some half-million people died under his watch, escalating during the Arab spring of 2011. In addition, millions of Syrians were displaced from their homes and became refugees in neighboring nations. With the fall of al-Assad in 2024, the true toll of torture, executions, and arbitrary arrests under his rule is only now becoming known.

A word of caution: Some readers will be tempted to write off such individuals as one-off examples of particularly evil character. But in truth, these three were all enabled by networks of officers and co-conspirators — people very much like you and I — who became complacent, cowardly, and shared in deep-seated guilt.

Great evil rarely begins with grand, monstrous acts — it grows from the seeds of casual evil. Small cruelties, indifference to suffering, and everyday moral compromises create an environment where atrocities incubate. When people dismiss minor injustices as insignificant or refuse to challenge wrongdoing in its infancy, they can passively enable far greater horrors. Apathy and self-interest pave the way for oppression, allowing evil to flourish unchallenged.

PROFOUND GOOD

By contrast, who among humanity has recently created the most good? Whose actions have alleviated suffering and fostered harmony? Competitors for this title are numerous and include the following.

David Livingstone (1813–1873) was born in abject poverty. As a 10-year-old child in Scotland, he worked in factories by day and was homeschooled by his father by night. Livingstone earned acceptance into the University of Oxford where he met individuals with a vision for the entire world, and as a young physician he settled in what is today the nation of South Africa. Immediately upon arrival, Livingstone was mauled by a lion. The injury crushed his brachial plexus, leading to permanent paralysis of his right arm, which hung limp at his side. But Livingstone was just getting started.

In his autobiography, Livingstone describes his first 10 years in Africa as the most fulfilling. He was raising his family, caring for those who were sick, and participating in his Christian community. Only after this did Livingstone begin his explorations of the continent. He wrote extensively about discovering Victoria Falls and tracing the origin of the Nile River. More significantly, he described the human character of African people, their feelings, dreams, and intellect. Livingstone's memoirs were avidly read throughout Western Civilization and his emphasis on the humanity of Africans is credited with the eventual abolishment of slavery throughout the British Empire.

Mother Teresa (1910–1997) had an early life that gave no extraordinary preview of her future influence. Born in modern-day Macedonia, a tiny nation just north of Greece, she joined as an adolescent a religious order and moved to India where she taught high school in Calcutta until age 38. Only in middle age did Mother Theresa leave her teaching position to found the Missionaries of Charity, an organization whose vision was to provide care for her Calcutta neighbors who were destitute, sick, and dying. Under her leadership, people who were previously considered less than human — including those with leprosy, HIV, and tuberculosis — were given homes, food, and basic medical care. Though she passed away in 1997, Mother Teresa's real-life example of compassion in action continues to inspire humanitarian service today.

Scott Armistead in the mountains of northern Pakistan, 2007. Credit: Scott Armistead.

Scott Armistead (1965–) deviated from the normal pathway of most Virginia physicians. Deeply concerned about the needs in South Asian, Dr. Armistead, his wife JoAnn, and their three small boys moved to Pakistan in 1999. They learned Urdu, the national language, and for the next 16 years they served at Bach Christian Hospital in the mountains north of Islamabad. During the changing security situation brought about by 9/11, they temporarily moved to the UAE but returned to Pakistan in 2003.

During the devastating earthquake of 2005, Dr. Armistead's hospital was on the front lines caring for the injured. During his years in Pakistan, he discovered his love for teaching and mentoring young Pakistani doctors. Returning to the United States in 2015 to care for family, he found many U.S. students eager to learn about global medicine. He started leading groups of medical students to serve at mission hospitals in Asia and Africa, with the intention of nurturing their sense of call to work among the needy of the world. He also initiated a weekly refugee gathering in Virginia through which students could form mentoring relationships with local refugees.

A word of encouragement: Some readers will be tempted to elevate individuals like these three as extraordinary and uncommon. However, the truth is that none of their accomplishments were achieved alone. Though they eventually became highly visible, their influence and success were largely built upon the work of associated donors, journalists, volunteers, administrators, and organizational leaders — skills that many of us today could readily contribute to.

Great good often begins with small, unnoticed acts of kindness. When kindness becomes habitual, it fosters trust and empathy. These actions can ripple outward, inspiring others and creating a community of compassion. Just as passivity can breed brutality, consistent care and decency can generate broad benevolence.

WHAT REPORT WILL WE GIVE?

What actions would we take, or not take, if we realized that one day we would give an account to the Creator for how we lived? More to the point, how would we treat others if we anticipated the requirement of explaining our actions to the One who controls our eternal destiny? A familiar response to such profound questions is to simply write them off, to assert that there is no Creator, no eternity, no judgment, no accountability. To take such a position is also to ignore two of the most profound subjects in the human experience: the origin of life and the Resurrection of Christ.

Exploring the origin of living things provokes questions about the possibility of a Designer. Examination of the evidence for Christ returning to life after execution supplies powerful confirmation for His claim to be that Designer. In this light, we do well to read carefully about the day of accountability forecast in Matthew 25 and then to act with extraordinary mercy and compassion toward people in our midst.

HOW DID LIFE BEGIN?

This question is relevant because it can be connected with the existence of a Supreme Being. If the origin of living things can be explained without reference to such a Being, this could be an argument for non-existence of the latter. But if the origin of life cannot be justified outside of action of a Supreme Being, this serves as strong reasoning that One must exist.

Even the "simplest" single living cell is complex almost beyond calculation. Stored within its genetic code is all the data necessary for its own function, metabolism, repair, and reproduction. Multicellular microorganisms, plants, and animals profoundly multiply that complexity. Today's most popular explanations for the origin of life center around four major phenomena: the first cell began as a random act of nature (spontaneous generation), followed by random genetic mutations, natural selection to favor the strongest of these mutations, and an enormous amount of time to allow for this process to develop into today's living creatures.

The origin of the first living cell is the most challenging of these phenomena. Is a random act of nature the most reasonable explanation? Many reputable scientists argue that, given the complex and highly ordered nature of living systems, the chance of life emerging purely by random processes is exceedingly low. An important element of their rationale is the concept of irreducible complexity. That is, if one essential function or component is missing, then the entire organism will not survive. At the cellular level, for example, if the cell lacks a membrane, the cell will collapse. Without the mitochondria, the cell will have no energy supply. Lacking the nucleus, most chemical functions of the cell never begin.

While the exact odds are difficult to calculate with precision, the probability of life beginning spontaneously is infinitesimally small. This assessment has stood the test of time. Louis Pasteur, the celebrated microbiologist, in 1859 debunked the concept of spontaneous generation. It has remained an unfounded explanation for the origin of life and continues to drive the alternate proposal that a Supreme Creator must exist.

DID CHRIST RETURN TO LIFE FROM DEATH?

Before discarding the future accountability event foretold in Matthew 25:32–40, we would also do well to consider the authority of the speaker. Most everyone agrees that Christ was a powerful moral teacher. But what makes Him unique compared to, say, Muhammed, Buddha, Abraham, or Marx? For one, we know where these four individuals are buried. Muhammad in Medina, Saudi Arabia. Buddha in Kushinagar, India. Abraham in Hebron, West Bank. Marx in North London, England. But where is Christ buried?

This, in fact, is the most important element of the life of Christ and the substance of the Christian faith: He returned to physical life three days after being killed. In this light, the Apostle Paul stated emphatically, "If there is no resurrection of the dead, then not even Christ has been raised. And if Christ has not been raised, our preaching is useless and so is your faith." 1 Corinthians 15:13-14. This profound claim, if true, should compel people the world over to listen carefully to His words.

Briefly, why would we consider it plausible that Christ indeed returned to life? Such a rationale is based on the following.

PROPHECIES FORETOLD CHRIST'S DEATH AND RESURRECTION.

The Book of Psalms chapter 22 (written between the ninth and the fifth centuries b.c.) and the Book of Isaiah chapter 53 (written between the seventh and sixth century b.c.) describe the people's reactions to Christ's arrest (mocking, spitting, staring), His silence, His manner of death, His burial in a rich man's tomb, and His purpose in allowing Himself to be killed. The New Testament Book of Matthew (composed between a.d. 60 and 130), and corroborated by contemporary Hebrew historians, records the fulfillment of these prophecies occurring in real time. These fulfilled prophecies add credibility to the extraordinary nature of Christ's resurrection.

DEATH BY CRUCIFIXION WAS ASSURED.

Some analysts have proposed that Christ never actually died. Rather, He only appeared to be dead. But the Roman executioners, who handled Christ, were experienced killers. Not only did the four writers of the Gospels confirm His death, but also contemporary historians, including Josephus, Tacitus, Lucian, Thallus, Mara Bar-Serapion, and the Talmud.

Even the American Medical Association contributed an analysis: "Clearly, the weight of historical and medical evidence indicates that Jesus was dead before the wound to his side was inflicted and supports the traditional view that the spear, thrust between his right rib, probably perforated not only the right lung but also the pericardium and heart and thereby ensured his death. Accordingly, interpretations based on the assumption that Jesus did not die on the cross appear to be at odds with modern medical knowledge."[2]

---

2 Edwards WD, Gabel WJ, Hosmer FE. "On the physical death of Jesus Christ." *JAMA.* 1986 Mar 21;255(11):1455-63. PMID: 3512867. https://pubmed.ncbi.nlm.nih.gov/3512867/

THE TOMB WAS UNEXPLAINABLY EMPTY.

Stones used to cover tomb entrances typically weighed some 4,000 pounds. The historical record documents that after Christ's burial, a Roman seal was placed on the tomb's entrance, and Roman law stated that breaking such a seal was punishable by death by crucifixion. Aware that Christ followers might attempt to steal His body, Roman guards were stationed to guard the tomb and were under threat of death if the site was breached.

How did the tomb become empty? Several explanations have been floated.

- Wrong Tomb Theory proposes that Christ followers mistakenly went to an empty tomb.
- Group Hallucination Theory suggests that they all suffered an identical delusion.
- Stolen-Body Theory proposes that Christ disciples, by all accounts cowardly, overcame the soldiers.
- Swoon-in-the-Tomb Theory explains that the not-quite-dead Christ pushed aside the stone and overcame the Roman guards.

The most plausible explanation is none of these. Rather, it is that an extraordinary event occurred by which Christ exited the tomb.

CHRIST'S DISCIPLES WERE RADICALLY TRANSFORMED

The actions of Christ's disciples before his arrest, trial, and execution were marked by fear. They fled, denied they knew Him, and hid from public sight, terrified that they too would be arrested, or worse. Yet, a few weeks later, these 11 men stood up on the streets of the capital city, Jerusalem, and boldly announced that Christ was alive. Furthermore, they urged, "… Repent and be baptized, every one of you, in the name of Jesus Christ for the forgiveness of your sins…." (Acts 2:38). So powerful was their message that some of the 3,000 people followed through by being baptized on just that first day.

The religious and political leaders of the city were greatly disturbed. They seized, jailed, and threatened the disciples, who replied, "… Which is right in God's eyes: to listen to you, or to him? You be the judges! As for us, we cannot help speaking about what we have seen and heard" (Acts 4:19–20).

What could possibly account for the dramatic reversal in the disciples' behavior? The most plausible explanation is that they witnessed Christ alive! The same man who days earlier predicted His death and Resurrection, who was executed and buried, now stood before them alive — thus powerfully confirming the truth of His message and compelling the disciples to speak out.

By contrast, if the Resurrection of Christ had not occurred, the disciples would have known it. Under threat of death for proclaiming Christ was alive, they would have recanted. Many people have died for a lie, believing it was the truth. But no one knowingly dies for what they know to be false.

ACCOUNTABLE

An explanation for the origin of life leads to the existence of a Creator. An explanation for the Resurrection of Christ leads to the authenticity of the Creator's words. These words foretell an upcoming event in which each person will give an account of themselves, an account based upon the compassion with which they have responded to people in need.

MORNING HAS BROKEN

The chilly morning following John the Baptist's surgery, just before dawn, I walked back toward the intensive care unit. My sleep had been fitful, thinking of how oxygen — always in short supply — might have helped to protect John the Baptist from brain injury. I also considered whether a different antibiotic would have been more effective. And, of course, I also mused over the fact that the cessation of the Angola Civil War continued to be the single most urgent intervention to save people like this man from certain death.

Entering the busy intensive care unit, I asked the nurse about the farmer. He replied, "Why don't you go and talk with him yourself?" I was startled!

My eyes immediately landed on what I expected to be an empty bed. But no. Instead, I saw a middle-aged man sitting up and enjoying his boiled cornmeal breakfast.

He too was startled. John the Baptist called out to me and asked in a perplexed voice, “Why are you, a foreigner, in Angola? Don’t you know we have a war going on? It’s very dangerous here!”

“I am overjoyed to see you awake!” I babbled, almost in disbelief at his recovery.

“I’m surprised, too,” said John the Baptist. “I was walking with a sack of seed corn, and the next thing I knew, I was blasted into the air. When I hit the ground, I was terrified to look. Blood was flowing out of my leg in torrents. I was so scared.” His voice was now trembling. “I took off my shirt and tied it tight around my leg. I cried out for help, but no one came. As my shock wore off, the pain became excruciating. As the sun set, I was sure that I would never see the morning again. But when I awoke, I was here at Kalukembe Hospital!”

Over the ensuing weeks, the farmer gradually became stronger. His amputation site healed nicely, and he learned to walk with crutches. After two months, his sons took their father home to his village and to his plot of land. The following year, he would return to Kalukembe Hospital to be fitted with a leg prosthesis.

On that day, I received a handwritten note from John the Baptist: “I am still baffled as to why you, a wealthy American, would come to help me and my Angolan people. A multitude of us have died

Nicholas Comninellis and Kalukembe Hospital Nurses, Angola 1989.
Credit: Author’s photo.

and will continue to die amid this conflict. In Angola you have no certainty you can save anyone's life. Yet, despite that uncertainty, you came nonetheless."

Chapter 4
Treasure Chest

A gentle tap on the window outside my bedroom was followed by a hushed, anxious voice. "Precisamos de ti imediatamente!" That is, "We need you immediately!" Nurses on night duty would never awaken me unless the situation was grave.

I rushed from home to the hospital, only 100 yards away, over a path known for snakes — and virtually every snake in Angola was deadly. Scanning the dark with my flashlight, I traded caution for speed.

I found her in labor and delivery, a woman in her 20s, malnourished, unconscious, and with a conspicuous double hump in her pregnant abdomen.

Her husband, Ezequiel, spoke rapidly in broken Portuguese:

> "My wife, she went into labor three days ago in our home. Her water broke and her contractions became stronger. But after a day, our baby did not come." His voice carried a pressured tone. "Our little town has no clinic, so I summoned the community health worker. She examined my wife and gave her medication to increase her labor. But after a second day, my wife lost consciousness, and her contractions stopped. When she would not wake up, I flagged down a passing truck. We have five little children at home. Can you help her?" he begged.

On the way to the operating room, I quickly stopped to change into surgical clothes and scrub my hands. I contemplated once more that trained midwives were rare in Angola — let alone physicians with obstetrics training. How desperately the nation needed individuals with maternal and newborn care skills, as well as a vision to serve people like Ezequiel's wife who had no means to repay them.

In the operating room, she was so comatose that little anesthesia was necessary. I made a midline, top-to-bottom incision in her abdomen, opened the facia, and there gazing up at me was a baby — a very deceased baby. Surrounding the little boy was an abdominal cavity filled with blood, amniotic fluid, and pus. I extracted the dead infant and evacuated the fluid, revealing the remnants of her ruptured uterus.

Surgery complete and now in recovery, I dosed her with intravenous fluid and antibiotics. Remarkably, the young woman began to move her extremities, breathe on her own, and call out for Ezequiel, who responded with joy at the sound of her voice.

In the washroom, I peeled off my soaked surgical clothes and soiled boots. I reflected to myself, This is what it means to die in childbirth. For millennia women have gone into labor, failed to progress for well-known reasons, and then continued to contract until overwhelmed by infection or succumbed to hemorrhage of a ruptured uterus. For a reality check of these dangers, we need only to look at nations like Angola, where armed conflict obstructs even the most basic maternal care.

Stopping by the recovery room, I saw that Ezequiel was now at his wife's bedside. More hopeful now, his voice was less strained and brow more relaxed. I mentioned to the man that I would intercede for his wife's healing.

Ezequiel straightened up attentively. "I know that God exists. I see signs of Him from every angle. But God is very impersonal and very far away. I don't think He can hear you."

"Please tell me more," I inquired.

"In the spirit world," Ezequiel continued, "there are evil spirits, who constantly make life difficult for us. They cause sickness and accidents, likely my wife's emergency, too. We also must contend with the spirits of our ancestors, pleasing them through shrines and small sacrifices. Hopefully, they will help defend us against the evil spirits." Ezequiel let out a sigh. "You see, Doctor, surely God cannot be bothered with all these details. My wife's illness, your prayer, the people working at your hospital, God has no time for your interest in such matters."

"The elders say, and I confirm," stressed Ezequiel, "that God lives on top of a mountain far away. He neither hears us nor cares for us."

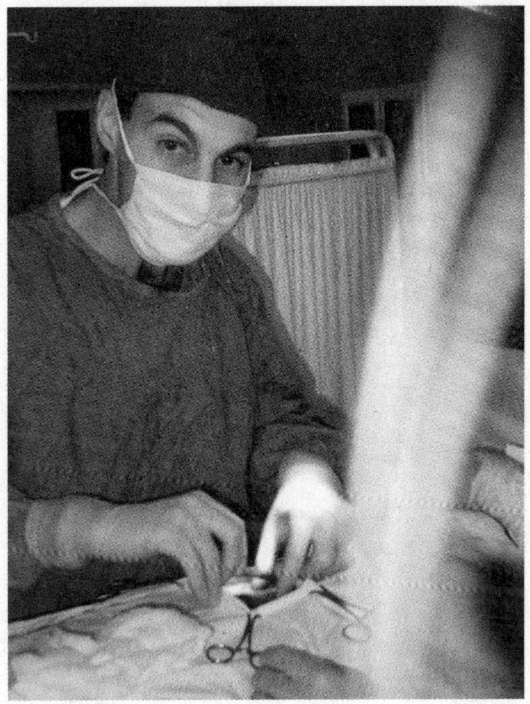

Nicholas Comninellis operating at Kalukembe Hospital, Angola 1990. Credit: Author's photo

TREASURE CHEST

A life focused on the welfare of others is extraordinary. The bar is high, especially since most individuals' intentions lie in amassing for themselves an assortment of positions, possessions, pleasures, and projects.

How can one hold fast to a people-first priority year after year and resist the constant pressure toward deviation and distraction? Put another way, how can we maintain with excellence the "chest" which contains and controls our treasures?

WHAT IS A "NORMAL" CHRISTIAN LIFE?

In this context the broader question is actually, What is a normal Christian life? Here the word normal means "expected" rather than what is "commonly observed." What is frequently viewed in society and labeled as "Christian" often has more to do with political alignment or norms of morality than with any definition recognizable within the pages of the Bible.

And what of the authority of the Bible? Just as the term "Christian" is manipulated to help support whatever the nefarious intentions of the user may be, so too is the power of the Bible frequently undermined to strip it of its authority.

Why do we today trust the Bible — the New Testament in particular — as the standard for what is expected of us rather than what any popular author, blogger, or YouTuber may say about the life and teachings of Christ? This is a consequential and perennial question. Even back in the first century, people were challenging the Christ narrative. What's more, Roman authorities via multiple edicts were ordering the destruction of Christian writings and the arrest of those identified as Christians. Among these was the Edict of Emperor Diocletain (303 a.d.) which ordered the destruction of sacred Christian writings. People who resisted were executed.[1] Christ's followers in that day did not want to die for their allegiance to just any writings. They wanted to know which had true authority!

A number of conventions, called synods, were held among leaders who represented the first churches. Among the best documented is the Synod of Hippo Regius in North Africa (393 a.d.) where 27 letters — today known as books — were selected.[2] These became the canon of the New Testament.

What criterion did synod leaders use to distinguish authoritative letters from the growing myriad of divergent writings? Three criteria were especially decisive.

---

1 "Diocletian and Christian Persecution," University of Chicago, accessed January 2, 2025. https://penelope.uchicago.edu/encyclopaedia_romana/hispania/diocletian.html

2 "The Canon of the New Testament," R Martinez. Accessed January 3, 2025. https://www.biblicaltheology.com/Research/MartinezR01.html

WAS IT WRITTEN BY A DISCIPLE OF JESUS OR A PERSON CLOSELY CONNECTED WITH THE EVENTS OF HIS LIFE?

Synod leaders placed trust in writers who were eyewitnesses. Gospel writers Matthew, Mark, and John, were disciples of Christ. Luke and Paul were their contemporaries and instrumental in establishing the first churches. As previously explored, these authors were threatened, jailed, flogged, and executed over their testimony regarding Christ.

WAS IT AUTHORITATIVE, CONTAINING GUIDANCE FOR RIGHTEOUS LIVING?

Synod leaders were convinced that letters must include the teachings of Christ and His disciples, providing clear and reliable instruction on how to live an upright life — unlike some of the circulating writings that claimed Christ's authority but contradicted the behavior He exemplified.

WAS IT ALREADY READ AND USED BY THE ORIGINAL FOLLOWERS OF CHRIST?

The existing recognition of the letters' credibility was a powerful endorsement of their content, especially because some of the readers lived in the time and place of Christ and likely heard Him speak themselves.

Today, people who claim allegiance to Christ continue to look to the New Testament to remind themselves of His normal expectations. This is especially vital for two reasons.

NORMAL EXPECTATIONS HELP US TO ASSESS OUR PERSONAL SPIRITUAL JOURNEY.

In this light, the Apostle Paul admonishes, "Examine yourselves to see whether you are in the faith; test yourselves. Do you not realize that Christ Jesus is in you—unless, of course, you fail the test? And I trust that you will discover that we have not failed the test." (2 Corinthians 13:5–6). Because the temptation toward distraction and deviation never ceases, the need for self-examination must continue daily throughout our lives.

NORMAL EXPECTATIONS GIVE US INSIGHT
TO DECIDE WITH WHOM TO PARTNER.

A people-first priority compels us to build relationships in many areas of life — work, business, dating, hobbies, and friendships. The success or failure of some relationships depends heavily upon whether we share a similar allegiance to Christ. A clear vision of normal expectations helps us to evaluate the dependability of these potential allies.

A useful model for assessing and developing a normal Christian life is through growing the content of our faith, the character of our faith, the community of our faith and the communication of our faith.

CONTENT OF OUR FAITH

Content of our faith refers to our beliefs, doctrines, and teachings. When we consider how Christianity differs or compares with secularism, Buddhism, Islam, or New Age beliefs, the subject inevitably centers on the core beliefs of these worldviews. A popular perspective around the globe is that all religions are ultimately the same — that all roads lead to God, or some similar pronouncements. But a thoughtful read of the New Testament reveals elements of Christianity that are radically unique. For example:

- Monotheism: There exists only one true God (Hebrews 11:6).
- Deity of Christ: Jesus Christ is God (John 4:48).
- Salvation by Grace: Forgiveness of sin is a gift received (Ephesians 2:8-9).
- Resurrection of Christ: Following execution, Christ returned to physical life (1 Corinthians 15:1–4).

The latter, explored in the previous chapter, is especially pivotal. Myths and legends mention Resurrection. But in recorded human history, no one has been documented to have died, been buried, and then returned to physical life. This historic event credibly supports the claims of Christ and the assurance affirmed by the Apostle Paul in 1 Corinthians 6:14, "By his power God raised the Lord from the dead, and he will raise us also."

How can we increase our understanding of and conviction about the content of what we believe? Examining the Bible, especially the New Testament Scriptures, is essential. Wonderful books, study guides, and videos are available to aid in such exploration. But none are more beneficial than actually reading the New Testament letters themselves. New followers of Christ often find this experience fascinating. Those of us who have followed Christ for a longer time continue to benefit from daily immersing our minds in the precepts of our faith, which helps us to fend off steady inclination toward diversion and disruption.

Another powerful means of better fathoming the content of our faith is to intentionally engage in conversation with people who do not necessarily agree with us. The relationships we enjoy with friends and colleagues provide natural opportunities to strike up a dialogue on spiritual subjects in the normal course of conversation. A useful approach is often to begin by asking an honest, nonjudgmental question like, "Could you please help me understand why you believe…?" As we genuinely listen to the perspectives of others, we often gain their trust and an opportunity to explain our own convictions in a way that will be well received.

CHARACTER OF OUR FAITH

What character qualities — fruit, if you will — should mark the lives of those who claim allegiance to Christ? This question today is especially pressing. Nowhere today are Christians more criticized than for the inconsistency between what we say we believe and how we actually behave. The frequent implosion of highly visible churches and Christian institutions due to the shameful conduct of their leaders emphasizes the dire consequences of failure to address the character of our faith. Preceding these moral lapses are often actions by leaders to insulate themselves from accountability and failure of those in their circles to call out warning signs.

Scripture is quite clear concerning character qualities that mark His authentic followers: "But the fruit of the Spirit is love, joy, peace, forbearance, kindness, goodness, faithfulness, gentleness and self-control. Against such things there is no law" (Galatians 5:22–23). We earnestly desire to see these qualities cultivated within ourselves.

New Testament Scripture also is replete with additional admirable features and actions that should mark the lives of Christ followers: praying without ceasing, rejoicing always, forgiving without retribution, showing hospitality, giving generously, honoring one another, demonstrating humility, being patient in affliction, and much more.

By contrast, Scripture also demarcates character qualities that distinguish those who are not following Christ. "The acts of the flesh are obvious: sexual immorality, impurity and debauchery; idolatry and witchcraft; hatred, discord, jealousy, fits of rage, selfish ambition, dissensions, factions and envy; drunkenness, orgies, and the like. I warn you, as I did before, that those who live like this will not inherit the kingdom of God" (Galatians 5:19–21). Every society is saturated with these dangerous elements, so much so that we can become indifferent to their influence or even drawn into their activities.

Does a defining principle exist that summarizes the qualities of a genuine follower of Christ — a through line that connects the ideal attributes of faith? In response to such a question Christ replied, "'Love the Lord your God with all your heart and with all your soul and with all your mind.' This is the first and greatest commandment. And the second is like it: 'Love your neighbor as yourself'" (Matthew 22:37–39). To remove any doubt about the extent to which we should love our neighbors, Christ also declared, "Greater love has no one than this: to lay down one's life for one's friends" (John 15:13).

Few of us will ever be faced with a crisis that requires us to literally sacrifice our lives for another. Far more common, and perhaps more difficult, is a day-by-day lifestyle of giving up our privileges so that others need not be hungry, thirsty, naked, sick, unhoused, or lonely. In doing so we convincingly display the character of faith in Christ.

How can we better cultivate the character of our faith? Increasing our understanding of what we believe (content) is valuable. Reserving time daily for prayer and spiritual reflection is vital. Actively seeking opportunities to serve others is exemplary. Being attentive to challenging situations and responding with grace is altogether excellent. Finally, perhaps no other element is more effective for developing our character than life in community.

COMMUNITY OF OUR FAITH

Community of our faith addresses how we interact with others who are following Christ. Human nature relentlessly pushes people to emphasize their cultural distinctives, their unique history, exclusive characteristics — all of which may create divisions between people. In contrast, Christ, in His final discourse instructed His disciples: "A new command I give you: Love one another. As I have loved you, so you must love one another. By this everyone will know that you are my disciples, if you love one another" (John 13:34–35). Our interactions as believers should be so rich and so generous that everyone who observes us sees Christ's character.

We benefit today from a glimpse of such interaction documented in Acts 2:44–47:

> "All the believers were together and had everything in common. They sold property and possessions to give to anyone who had need. Every day they continued to meet together in the temple courts. They broke bread in their homes and ate together with glad and sincere hearts, praising God and enjoying the favor of all the people. And the Lord added to their number daily those who were being saved."

Especially instructive are the principles expressed in this description of the early church:

- Everything in common. They freely shared.
- Giving to anyone in need. They expressed concern through generosity.
- Meeting together. They genuinely enjoyed one another's companionship.
- Worshiping God. As a group they expressed gratefulness.
- Outward influence. Observers wanted the same faith they had.

Christians must be vigilant to keep in sight such virtues as healthy indicators of their life in community. Why? Because standard measures of worldly success — like buildings, financial status, numbers of participants — can come to permeate church life, and even be interpreted as meaning that we are being rewarded by God for our faith. History is replete with accounts of such misinterpretation. In the fifth century, for example, when Christianity became the state religion of Rome, the political success of the faith became "proof" that Christians were correct and following God — which entirely contradicts the notion of the narrow way preached by Jesus.

We see a similar mixing of worldly measures of success in the 21st century. Western Civilization has witnessed a demographic decline in the number of people who identify as Christians. Many churches have closed, and congregations have shrunk or consolidated. Some followers of Christ interpret this phenomenon as a spiritual failure of Christianity. However, Christ never suggested that the absolute number of His followers would indicate success. If this were actually the case, it would stand to reason that He would have trained more than just 12 disciples. Rather, consider again how He defined successful community of faith: "… As I have loved you, so you must love one another. By this everyone will know that you are my disciples, if you love one another" (John 13:34–35). This standard should be our measure of success, even though it does not appeal to today's predominant favorable outcomes as enumerated by quantitative data.

The community of our faith should not stand alone. Ideally, it should be closely linked with both Content and Character. As we interact with other followers of Christ, we together analyze and increase our understanding of our beliefs. Similarly, in the context of community we also encourage one another to develop the attributes of Christ-like character and serve as watchmen, sounding an alarm if we notice behavior that suggests any of us may be straying.

COMMUNICATION OF OUR FAITH

What is the expected influence of one who's content of faith is true, who's character of faith is upstanding, and who's community of faith is exceptional? Outsiders may observe such a person with respect and admiration. But they often nevertheless remain in the dark regarding the Christ who inspires he or she. Therefore, the communication of our faith is also paramount.

At times, the message of Christ will compel a spiritually lost, nonbelieving person to make an enduring faith decision the very first time it is heard. But this is the exception. More commonly, over a period of months or years, this person hears the Good News multiple times, interacts off and on with people already following Christ, takes in Christian videos or podcasts, opens the Bible for themselves, and even engages in worship or service alongside Christ-following people.

What can we do to encourage such a person's spiritual exploration? Most fundamental is that our own lives be closely in sync with Christ. As our faith's content, character, and community continues to grow, so does the likelihood of our illuminating influence. As we continue engaging this person, other opportunities will likely arise to more directly communicate the Good News.

What is the Good News? How can this be best summarized? Clearly, the message may need to be adjusted for the context or for the felt need of the listener. In short, the Good News is forgiveness for every trespass (sin) and the promise of eternal life through turning away from trespass and obeying Christ - all of this proven by Him, a dead man, returning to life.

By intentionally, prayerfully, engaging in conversation with lost people we can use these opportunities to share the Good News in ways that are both tactful and effective. But we must make ourselves available. This may mean reserving extra time after work, during lunch, at the gym, during study period, or in the midst of our favorite activities to be ready for conversations.

Sharing our own personal story towards trust in Christ is a natural and uniquely powerful way to begin. As people respond favorably, a next step is to invite these friends to read the New Testament together with us. As we sit side-by-side, comments and questions will naturally arise that help the people better understand what it means to follow Christ. An added benefit of this experience is that we, too, often increase our own understanding and ability to better communicate in the future.

Communicating our faith can be an amazing adventure, filled with growing to know and deeply value other people. Communicating our faith is also part of a process for which we ourselves may not see the long-term outcome. The apostle Paul references this truth when speaking about sharing the Good News in the city of Corinth, writing, "I planted the seed, Apollos watered it, but God has been making it grow" (1 Corinthians 3:6). That we, too, may play a role in the spiritual growth of another is one of life's greatest privileges.

WHERE OUR TREASURES ARE STORED

The inner being of each person — our treasure chest — is a pivotal space. It guards and guides how we handle each treasure entrusted to us. Therefore, we strive to ensure the security and resilience of our individual treasure chests. A useful model for doing so, for assessing and developing a normal Christian life, is through growing the content of our faith, the character of our faith, the community of our faith, and the communication of our faith.

GOD CAME DOWN

Ezequiel's wife's wounds were very slow to heal, compounded by pre-existing anemia and malnutrition. More than once I drained pus from abscesses within her abdomen and on her surgical incision. Through it all, Ezequiel was at her side. He fed her, bathed her, and assisted her with walking. Between caregiving duties, I frequently noticed Ezequiel on the hospital veranda, listening intently as the chaplain each morning read the Bible and described the Good News: forgiveness for every trespass and the promise of eternal life through turning away from sin and obeying Christ — all of this proven by Him, a dead man, returning to life.

As the weeks progressed the sound of gunfire became more frequent. Combat aircraft, rarely seen before, begin overflying the area several times each day, sending waves of anxiety through patients, professionals, and townspeople. News from outside was sparse, but a visit to Kalukembe Hospital by the Swiss ambassador alerted us to impending battles. Then, the artillery booms were followed by explosions that grew closer night by night. Still, the staff remained at our posts.

Trucks rumbled into the rotunda daily, offloading scores of civilians and injured soldiers from both sides. Most had injuries to their extremities, fractures, and bullet wounds. But few arrived with trauma to their head, chest, or abdomen. Why? These people usually died on the spot. Civilians were not immune: children with shrapnel embedded in their flesh, women with crush injuries from their homes collapsing, and young men routinely shot as they fled military inscription. Gradually, I realized that after two years in Angola, my colleagues and I would eventually be forced to evacuate.

Ezequiel, too, was aware of the impending need to take his recovering wife and flee. As we spoke about this one afternoon, he added, "I was wrong about God. The chaplain explained how Christ came, lived among us, shared in our suffering, died, and rose from the dead."

"You were already familiar with the Good News?" I inquired.

"Yes, but I'd never seen it in action," explained Ezequiel. "Here at Kalukembe Hospital, my wife and I received mercy from people in whom I can clearly see the character of Christ. To me, this is the most compelling reason to believe that God really is no longer on a mountaintop far away. He indeed cares, actually listens, and already came down to us."

Angolan chaplin nurse sharing the Good News about Christ with her patients and their children prior to each day's clinic. Angola, 1990. Credit: Author's photo.

Part Three:

What Will You Do Right Now with Your Treasure?

... a man going on a journey ...called his servants and entrusted his wealth to them (Matthew 25:14).

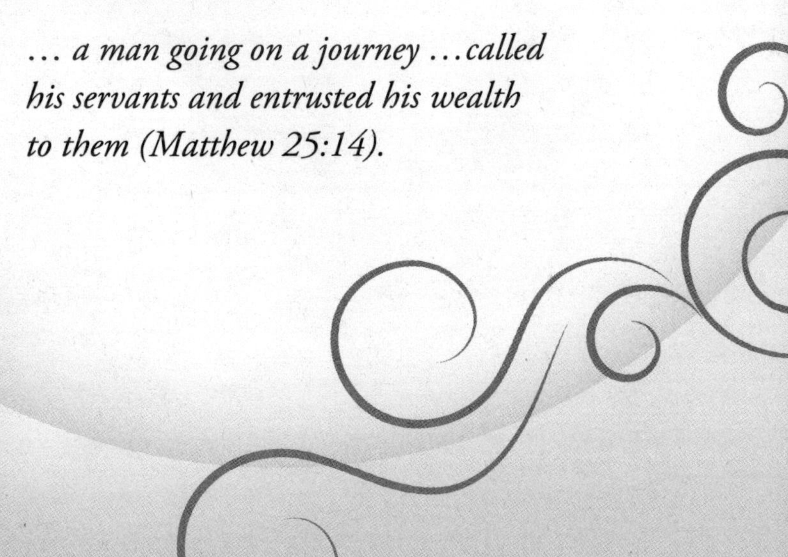

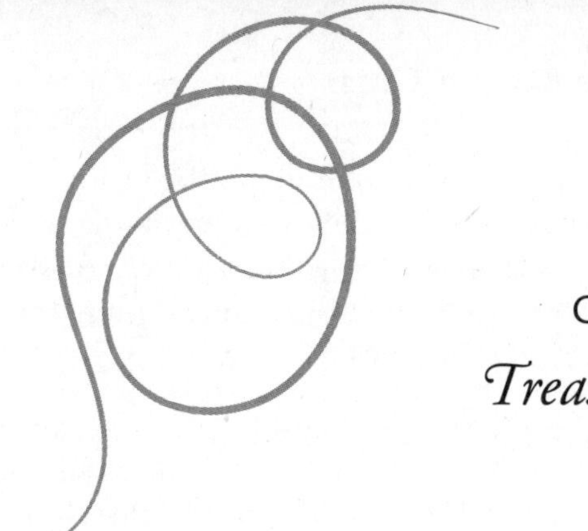

Chapter 5

Treasure Map

At Park Hill High School, just north of Kansas City, Missouri, I was totally engaged. I participated in debate, track, student government, symphonic band, and even did a little studying. To earn spending money, I taught guitar lessons. During two summers, I lived with my grandmother on the Greek island of Lemnos. But as each summer ended, I was anxious to jump back into life at Park Hill. Still, I realized that high school would not last long. So, I pondered, What shall I do with my life?

Aeronautical engineering was fascinating, but my math skills were poor. Music was inspiring, but I was not especially gifted. A role in our family business was offered, but commerce held little meaning for me. Graduation was looming and my anxiety grew.

A profound experience shaped my decision-making process as a young man. My spiritual upbringing was within the confines of a highly structured religious system, where adherence to customs and culture was paramount. At school, by contrast, I met a circle of friends whose approach to spiritual life was extremely refreshing.

Nicholas Comninellis 1976 Park Hill High School Graduation photo. Credit: Author's photo.

They prayed together in a classroom each morning, shared with one another what they were learning from the Bible over lunchtime, and gathered in the evenings to enjoy worship songs together. Above all, they were very friendly. Soon, I too joined in pledging my own allegiance to Christ.

THE PARABLE OF THE BAGS OF GOLD

In those early months I devoured the New Testament. The virtue expressed in 1 Corinthians 13 was among the most inspiring things I had ever read. The poetic purity of 1 John filled my soul with joy. And within Matthew 25, I discovered a preview of future accountability to Christ that would guide my life, saying:

> "… It will be like a man going on a journey, who called his servants and entrusted his wealth to them. To one he gave five bags of gold, to another two bags, and to another one bag, each according to his ability. Then he went on his journey. The man who had received five bags of gold went at once and put his money to work and gained five bags more. So also, the one with two bags of gold gained two more. But the man who had received one bag went off, dug a hole in the ground and hid his master's money.
>
> "After a long time the master of those servants returned and settled accounts with them. The man who had received five bags of gold brought the other five. 'Master,' he said, 'you entrusted me with five bags of gold. See, I have gained five more.'
>
> "His master replied, 'Well done, good and faithful servant! You have been faithful with a few things; I will put you in charge of many things. Come and share your master's happiness!'
>
> "The man with two bags of gold also came. 'Master,' he said, 'you entrusted me with two bags of gold; see, I have gained two more.'
>
> "His master replied, 'Well done, good and faithful servant! You have been faithful with a few things; I will put you in charge of many things. Come and share your master's happiness!'

> "Then the man who had received one bag of gold came. 'Master,' he said, 'I knew that you are a hard man, harvesting where you have not sown and gathering where you have not scattered seed. So I was afraid and went out and hid your gold in the ground. See, here is what belongs to you.'
>
> "His master replied, 'You wicked, lazy servant! So you knew that I harvest where I have not sown and gather where I have not scattered seed? Well then, you should have put my money on deposit with the bankers, so that when I returned I would have received it back with interest.
>
> "'So take the bag of gold from him and give it to the one who has ten bags. For whoever has will be given more, and they will have an abundance. Whoever does not have, even what they have will be taken from them. And throw that worthless servant outside, into the darkness, where there will be weeping and gnashing of teeth'" (Matthew 25:14–30).

ONE BAG

This Parable of the Bags of Gold is also widely known as the Parable of the Talents. A talent at that time was a monetary unit worth about 20 years' wages, as earned by a laborer. So, by this definition, a bag of gold is an understatement. Each bag would have to include at least $1 million in USD currency today,[1] for according to a quick search on the Bureau of Labor website, blue collar workers in the United States earned between $50,000 and $80,000 in 2023.[2]

In this account, the most precarious status was that of the servant who received one bag of gold. At the outset, he was already one of the master's most trusted administrators. For this reason, the master rewarded this servant with his trust and the responsibility of managing his wealth. But the servant, fearful of consequences for failure, decidedly withdrew from taking any risks whatsoever. The result? In the judgment of the master, this servant's unfaithfulness was so profound that he was expelled from the master's kingdom.

---

1 The Parable of the Talents (Matthew 25:14-30). Theology of Work Project. https://www.theologyofwork.org/new-testament/matthew/living-in-the-new-kingdom-matthew-18-25/the-parable-of-the-talents-matthew-2514-30/. Accessed March 8, 2025.

2 Model Wage Estimates. U.S. Bureau of Labor Statistics. https://www.bls.gov/mwe/factsheets/blue-collar-jobs-factsheet.htm. Accessed March 8, 2025.

What is the most important implication of the one-bag-of-gold servant for us today? Warning against inaction. Hoarding the treasure entrusted to us is equated with unfaithfulness to Christ and punished by separation from Him forever. This stark warning should provoke careful, serious, and periodic reflection within us, lest we squander the resources the Master entrusts to us.

TWO BAGS

On the day of judgment, the man with two bags of gold reported, "… Master, you entrusted me with two bags of gold; see, I have gained two more," and the elated Master replied, "Well done, good and faithful servant! You have been faithful with a few things; I will put you in charge of many things. Come and share your master's happiness!" (Matthew 25:22–23).

The two-bags-of-gold servant represents the normal Christian life, the standard expectations for everyone who claims allegiance to the Master. We consciously evaluate our assets, consider our opportunities, and deliberately take action so that our account shows steady growth.

Yet many followers of Christ do not follow through on basic expectations. Why? Because of distraction and deviation. We become distracted with the immediate concerns of daily life. Auto maintenance, an overdue bill, a disobedient child — all of these are reasonable responsibilities. But without parameters, they can consume our strength and time. We may also be led astray by societal standards that tempt our allegiance away from Christ. Political affiliations and social causes, while at times ethical and just, can also become so compelling that they supplant our loyalty to Him.

FIVE BAGS OF GOLD

The five-bags-of-gold servant, similar to the one entrusted with two bags of gold, was greeted with the Master's accolades for loyalty and his expressions of pleasure. According to the opportunities given, each of these servants performed well. They took action based upon the Master's instructions and, over time, successfully completed His directive.

What is the implication of this parable for us today? The account of the Five Bags of Gold clearly refers to the future judgment of each follower of Christ, stressing the accountability for how we use the resources entrusted to us. Many of us today have already received several bags of gold. We possess physical health, mental prowess, education, occupational skills, life experience, affirmation from family, honor from friends and colleagues, and spiritual insight and discernment.

TWO BAGS OR FIVE BAGS — WHAT IS THE DIFFERENCE?

Some may be tempted to see the distribution of two bags to one servant and five bags to another as a sign of God's preferential favor to one over the other. We must be cautious against such an interpretation. God judges us based on what we have been given and expects us to grow it accordingly. The servant who gained only two bags more is just as worthy as the one who gained five more.

For context, consider the account of the Widow's Offering. Christ and His disciples were on location at the temple in Jerusalem: "As Jesus looked up, he saw the rich putting their gifts into the temple treasury. He also saw a poor widow put in two very small copper coins. 'Truly I tell you,' he said, 'this poor widow has put in more than all the others. All these people gave their gifts out of their wealth; but she out of her poverty put in all she had to live on'" (Luke 21:1–4).

Christ's analysis of these offerings highlights the importance of action proportionate to the resources allocated to us. The widow's offering — "she out of her poverty put in all she had to live on" — exemplifies utter faith and dependence on God, in stark contrast with the self-sufficiency of the wealthy donors. Her act serves as a lesson that value in God's eyes is not measured by the absolute amount received and invested but by the spirit and faithfulness with which it is used — whether our money, time, effort, or devotion.

I'M ALL IN

Of course, we do not simply want to hoard these treasures or spend them only on our pleasures. Rather, we do want to invest wisely the riches we possess. To think or act otherwise would be to deny our allegiance to Christ, His authority over our lives, and our coming accountability to Him.

The challenge for most of us is to move beyond being ordinary treasure managers — not risking too much, not enduring unnecessary stress, as we handle the resources temporarily assigned to us. The challenge is for us to become exceptional treasure managers — willing to risk it all, shouldering the accompanying stress, as we strive to honor Christ with the limited time we have. To apply a phrase from the world of poker, "I'm all in!"

The Apostle Paul expresses similar sentiment in his letter to Titus, a church leader of his time: "… Jesus Christ, who gave himself for us to redeem us from all wickedness and to purify for himself a people that are his very own, eager to do what is good." (Titus 2:13–14). Paul is emphasizing that in light of the dramatic, transformative power of Christ in our lives, we will fervently follow through with actions of obedience and mercy.

WHERE DO WE GO FROM HERE?

Time is one of our most precious treasures. We have only a limited supply — about 25,000 days in the average person's life. How can we who are "All in" best use our time and other resources to honor Christ? What will we choose? What path shall we take?

These were the very questions I wrestled with as I approached the end of high school — the same kinds of questions we all face at various points throughout our lives, such as:

- How can I learn to control my temper?
- Will I continue to trust Christ though I may be rejected by my friends?
- Whom shall I marry?
- How far should I live from my parents?
- What church will I participate in?
- Which close friends will I choose?
- How can I best reach my nonbelieving friends for Christ?
- What occupation shall I pursue?
- Where should I work?

When we ask such questions, in reality we are deciding how to use our treasures in specific situations.

HOW DOES GOD GUIDE?

We need God's help to make the best decisions possible. In fact, there may be danger without it. Proverbs 14:12 warns us, "There is a way that appears to be right, but in the end it leads to death." So, Christ's followers often talk about the will of God. How we understand God's direction can greatly influence our attitudes (fatalistic or enthusiastic), our decision-making process (passive or active), and our actions (apathetic or assertive).

For this reason, Paul emphasized: "Therefore do not be foolish, but understand what the Lord's will is" (Ephesians 5:17), and later, "… We continually ask God to fill you with the knowledge of his will through all the wisdom and understanding that the Spirit gives" (Colossians 1:9). God will help guide us. Let's examine two important ways.

GOD'S GENERAL GUIDANCE — PRICELESS AND AVAILABLE

God provides us with general guidance — general in that it is available to each person. Sometimes the terms "universal" or "moral" guidance are also used. The best way to receive God's general guidance is to absorb the teachings in the Bible, as 2 Timothy 3:16–17 explains: "All Scripture is God-breathed and is useful for teaching, rebuking, correcting and training in righteousness, so that the servant of God may be thoroughly equipped for every good work."

Some of God's general guidance includes:

- Give cheerfully to people in need (2 Corinthians 9:7)
- Resolve conflicts between one another (Matthew 5:7–9)
- Be careful with our speech (James 3:9–10)
- Pray for one another's spiritual growth (Colossians 1:9–10)
- Care for people less fortunate than ourselves (James 1:27)
- Stay sexually pure (1 Thessalonians 4:1–3)
- Meet together and encourage other followers of Christ (Hebrews 10:25)
- Be thankful to God (1 Thessalonians 5:18)

God has already provided essential directions to guide us. But we must thoroughly explore the Bible to discover them, and then intentionally orient our lives accordingly.

GODS INDIVIDUAL GUIDANCE — PRECIOUS AND RARE

The Bible does not, however, address the details of every situation. It does not tell us specifically whom to marry, exactly where to go to school, or what particular profession to pursue. Neither does it reveal where to live, where to establish our fellowship, where to go on vacation, or whether we should go on vacation at all. Does God help us with these kinds of individual decisions?

The Bible contains reports of God giving people specific, individual instructions via an audible voice, vision, or a dream, telling them whom to marry, where to live, whom to meet, where to travel, and what to say (Matthew 1:20, 2:13, 2:20; Acts 10, 16:9–10, 18:9–11, 22:17–21, 27:23–25). For example, in Acts 9 we read about Christ appearing to Paul in a vision and telling him to go into Damascus. About the same time, Christ also appeared to a man named Ananias, telling him exactly where to find Paul. When the two men met, Ananias showed Paul how to become a follower of Christ. Clearly, Christ orchestrated this specific event!

Sometimes God guides individuals in very specific ways. However, most accounts described in the Bible were accompanied by some supernatural sign. When God directed, His voice was unmistakable — there was no doubt about who was speaking!

"GOD TOLD ME TO"

A word of caution: At times Christians may use the language of the will of God to justify their own selfish actions, defending that, "God told me to do it." We must approach such claims very carefully — taking into account the context, our relationship with the person, and the nature of what they claim God told them. Thoughtful ways to respond include:

- Respect and Listen — Show respect for their belief and listen attentively. You might reply, "That's interesting! Can you tell me more about how you feel God spoke to you?" This may help you to better understand their perspective.

- Compare with Scripture — Clarify their claim by gently asking, "How does that align with what the Bible teaches?" God's guidance never contradicts Scripture.
- Discernment from Others — If their claim involves major decisions or actions that seem questionable, you may ask, "With whom have you discussed it for confirmation?"
- Encourage Personal Reflection — If you feel uneasy, you can respond, "How long have you prayed about that?" or "That's something worth praying more about."

Your response should be both gracious and discerning, aiming to encourage wisdom and biblical alignment, as well as preserving your relationship with the person to provide future opportunities for interaction.

HOW SHOULD WE DECIDE?

God may communicate with us in some extraordinary way, and if He does, we should certainly follow through. But based on all reports today, individual, supernatural guidance is uncommon. So, what should be the basis for our decisions? The general guidance found in the Bible!

Let's look at how some of the first Christians made specific decisions.

First, we find a problem in the church at Jerusalem (Acts 6:1–6). Not everyone was receiving their share of food. The leaders asked the people to choose seven men to resolve the conflict. "This proposal pleased the whole group," so they choose the men who seemed most qualified.

Later, we find two men, Barnabas and Saul, in the church at Antioch. They had recently returned from an expedition during which they started several new churches. One day, Paul said to Barnabas, "…Let us go back and visit the believers in all the towns where we preached the word of the Lord and see how they are doing " (Acts 15:36). They both thought this was a great idea, so they planned the trip and set off.

In another example, the first churches had a question about which foods could be consumed (1 Corinthians 8, 10:23–33). Paul told them to decide for themselves, but to be considerate of one another's feelings. Paul made it clear that most decisions are simply up to us, and that we are responsible for the outcome (Romans 14:1–6,10,12).

Many examples show Christians making individual decisions (Acts 11:27–30, 17:16–17, 20:16;1 Corinthians 6:1–6, 16:1–9; Philippians 2:25-26; 1 Thessalonians 3:1–2). Their pattern was to apply Jesus' teachings to each situation, and then make up their minds, often expressing their decisions with phrases such as: "We thought it best," "I thought it necessary," "It seemed good," or simply, "I have decided." These examples offer guidance for us today. We must develop our decision-making skills so we can wisely apply Jesus' teaching to each situation we face. Such freedom of choice has been part of God's plan from the beginning.

LIFE IN THE GARDEN

In Genesis, for example, we read, "The LORD God took the man and put him in the Garden of Eden to work it and take care of it. And the Lord God commanded the man, "You are free to eat from any tree in the garden; but you must not eat from the tree of the knowledge of good and evil, for when you eat from it you will certainly die" (Genesis 2:15–17). Thousands of blooming trees and bushes must have surrounded Adam. For breakfast, he could select from strawberries, grapes, or nuts. At lunchtime, options included apples, celery, or lettuce. For supper, the menu could include clementines, sweet corn, or sweet potatoes. Everything was within bounds except for the fruit of that one dangerous tree.

The parallel for us today is unmistakable. We enjoy enormous freedom of choice within the parameters of God's general guidance, which He established for our benefit and protection. Whom we marry, what we study, and where we choose to live — absent supernatural revelation — are our own decisions. God gives us tremendous freedom and responsibility to select for ourselves, within the framework of His general guidance.

Does freedom of choice imply that God doesn't care about our "small" affairs? No. Quite the opposite. God loves us, forgives us, gives us strength and eternal life. He cares about even our "small" decisions. This is why He provides us with general guidance. But God also gives us the privilege and responsibility to choose for ourselves in most situations. God has called us to peace, to love, and to share His message. It is up to us to work out the details.

FREE BUT NOT ALONE

Within God's general guidance, we enjoy enormous freedom of choice. But even with this freedom we are not alone. God offers us wisdom. By wisdom I mean, "The power to see, and the inclination to choose, the best and highest goal, together with the surest means of attaining it."[3]

Wisdom is a precious treasure — more valuable than money or skill. Proverbs 3:13–14 tells us, "Blessed are those who find wisdom, those who gain understanding, for she is more profitable than silver and yields better returns than gold."

Where can we find wisdom? By going to God — the Creator of wisdom. He wants to give it, but first we must ask. The Bible records this promise: "… if you call out for insight and cry aloud for understanding, and if you look for it as for silver and search for it as for hidden treasure, then you will understand the fear of the LORD and find the knowledge of God. For the LORD gives wisdom, and from his mouth come knowledge and understanding" (Proverbs 2:3–6).

What is the difference between godly wisdom and academic research with scientific discovery? The latter can yield significant progress that benefits humanity. Consider, for example, the millions of lives that have been saved since the introduction of the measles vaccine in 1963. But academic research with scientific discovery has also produced horrific results, like the invention of nerve gases and the Tuskegee Syphilis Study. By contrast, genuine understanding and wisdom from God lead to genuine compassion and sacrifice on behalf of one another.

King Solomon was known for his great wisdom. But in the beginning, wisdom was not his. Then, as a young man, Solomon became ruler of ancient Israel, an enormous responsibility for which he was unprepared. So, Solomon asked God for wisdom — rather than for possessions, health, or political victories. God responded by granting Solomon more wisdom than any person of his time, and Solomon's leadership in Israel was unsurpassed (1 Kings 3).

---

3 J.I. Packer, *Knowing God* (Downers Grove, IL: Intervarsity Press, 1973).

Like Solomon, we need to ask for wisdom, and apply God's general guidance. Much of the Bible's advice about excellent decision-making can be summed up in the mnemonic **POPCORN**:

P O P C O R N Decision Making	
P	- **P**ray for Wisdom
O	- **O**ptions Listed
P	- **P**ros Considered
C	- **C**ons Considered
O	- **O**pen Your Bible
R	- **R**ecommendations Heard
N	- **N**o Hurry!

Before you begin, be certain you understand the question. What exactly needs to be decided? Write out the question if necessary. Sometimes more than one issue is being considered. For example, decisions about career choice and education or job selection and where to raise a family, are often lumped together. Considering them separately may be more expedient.

PRAY FOR WISDOM — P O P C O R N

The first step in making any good decision is to ask God for wisdom. Share with God your feelings and thoughts about the issue. Then simply ask Him to help you, for God promises to do so (James 1:5–6).

One special benefit of this approach is peace. Throughout my experience in China, in Angola, and in the United States I have discovered that even people who do not consider themselves religious or spiritual nevertheless tell me that they pray. They describe a sense of clarity and calm that often results. Philippians 4:6–7 assures us all, "Do not be anxious about anything, but in every situation, by prayer and petition, with thanksgiving, present your requests to God. And the peace of God, which transcends all understanding, will guard your hearts and your minds in Christ Jesus." We can better relax when we trust Him with our concerns.

OPTIONS LISTED — P O P C O R N

Next, list all options, answers, or alternatives that come to mind. Schedule a brainstorming session protected from interruption, and use the opportunity to intentionally open your imagination. New choices often come to us after we eliminate preconceived notions.

Ask others to join you both in praying for wisdom and exploring possibilities.

PROS AND CONS CONSIDERED — P O P C O R N

Every option has advantages and disadvantages. The sooner we recognize them; the sooner we can choose the best alternative. Spencer Johnson, author of *The One Minute Manager,* put it like this: "Our poor decisions were based on illusions we believed at the time, and our better decisions on realities we recognized in time."[4]

Gather all the information possible about your options. Then examine each option in light of that information and visualize yourself in those potential situations. For each option, create a list of corresponding pros and cons.

Have you found an option that seems perfect in every way? Be careful. Even the best options are accompanied by some downsides. If you don't see any, more examination is certainly wise.

As you consider your options, be sure to take into account your resources. Each of us has certain skills, interests, time, and financial constraints. Do you have the resources necessary for each option? Be honest with yourself.

Also consider your relationships. Few decisions have no impact on others. How will each alternative affect your relationship with Christ, your family, fellow believers, your work, and those who may be far from the knowledge of God?

Jesus stresses the importance of considering the pros and cons, saying, "Suppose one of you wants to build a tower. Won't you first sit down and estimate the cost to see if you have enough money to complete it? For if you lay the foundation and are not able to finish it, everyone who sees it will ridicule you, saying, 'This person began to build and wasn't able to finish.'" (Luke 14:28–30). Effort and time are required to envision the implications of each option. But when we take this approach, our ultimate choices will be superior.

OPEN YOUR BIBLE — P O P C O R N

Next, explore the Bible for guidance that may inform your decision. You might, for example, be considering whether or not to join a

4 Kenneth Blanchard and Spencer Johnson, *The One Minute Manager* (New York, NY: HarperCollins, 1983).

church. Hebrews 10:24–25 has compelling advice. You could be struggling with sexual temptation. First Corinthians 6:18–20 gives important counsel.

If you find no specific instructions for your situation, look for a principle that applies. You may, for example, be considering how to use vacation time. The Bible does not directly address your specific situation. However, Philippians 2:3–4 advises us to put the welfare of others before ourselves, and Mark 6:31 points out the importance of personal rest. These principles, among others in God's general guidance, may help you decide what is best for your situation.

RECOMMENDATIONS HEARD — P O P C O R N

Asking for advice is not a sign of weakness, but rather evidence of wisdom. Proverbs 15:22 reveals that, "Plans fail for lack of counsel, but with many advisers they succeed." Proverbs 19:20 urges, "Listen to advice and accept discipline, and in the end you will be counted among the wise." A degree of healthy humility is required to seek out guidance from experts, but the investment often proves invaluable.

It is especially important is get recommendations from people to whom we are responsible — friends, professors, employers, pastors, and others who know us well and who may be impacted by our choices. Do not neglect to ask parents for their input (Proverbs 6:20). While we may be well beyond their legal authority, they know us very well and usually have our best interests at heart. Soliciting counsel from those who may not necessarily agree with us is also wise, for they may provide an important perspective we have not yet considered.

Finally, asking for advice is a vital way of honoring people. It communicates, "You are important, and I can learn from you." It also aids in enlisting their support, which can be essential if you later need their input or assistance once again in the future. On the balance, however, we must be careful not to make decisions simply to please others. We listen to their counsel, but we must ultimately choose for ourselves. Otherwise, we may eventually feel manipulated or suppressed, missing out on the self-respect that comes from taking responsibility for how we manage our own lives.

NO HURRY — POPCORN

Good decisions demand concentration and time. The more energy we invest, the better the outcome will be. Proverbs 21:5 agrees: "The plans of the diligent lead to profit as surely as haste leads to poverty." Emotionally charged choices, like those surrounding romance or major purchases, especially call for unhurried evaluation. When we are rushed, it is impossible to consider all the factors and implications, as U.S. President Dwight D. Eisenhower stressed in his 1954 address to the Second Assembly of the World Council of Churches, "The urgent is seldom important and the important seldom urgent."[5]

Instead, take time to test and probe the options. Begin early and proceed slowly. Major decisions should only be made when we feel rested and can focus our attention. When we allow ample time, confusion tends to fade, and our choices become more clear.

DECISION TIME

When an airplane is in flight, the pilot rarely relies upon any single method of navigation, since any may be faulty. Instead, he or she will use several simultaneous techniques: GPS, radio beacons, landmarks, radar reports, clock and compass, and more. The pilot cross-checks them against one another to assure the airplane is indeed on course. Similarly, we do well to employ multiple guidelines and all available wisdom in making our decisions.

Some people fail to make choices because they are looking for a perfect option, one that is entirely good in every way. But even with the best decisions, some negative outcome will often result. Most decisions are not ones of absolute right or wrong. Instead, we are more often confronted with issues that may be accompanied by numerous pros and cons on either side. In these situations, the best we can do is to choose the option that we believe will lead to maximum good and minimum negative repercussions.

WHAT ABOUT PEACE?

Ours is a God of peace (1 Corinthians 14:33), and peace is one result of Christ's influence in our lives (Galatians 5:22). Our decisions

---

5 *Public Papers of the Presidents of the United States,* Dwight D. Eisenhower, 1954. Pg. 737

should generate a sense of contentment, which is often an inner signal that we have come to a genuine resolution. While some anxiety surrounding big decisions is normal — such as before a wedding, the first day of school, or starting a new job — a persistent sense of peace about a choice is an important indicator.

The opposite of peace is doubt. Decisions should be acts of faith and confidence, not symptoms of confusion. When we are unsettled, we best proceed cautiously, keeping our options open, and continuing to carefully evaluate before making a commitment.

Furthermore, a sense of peace is not always the determining factor. Followers of Christ have felt anxiety while doing the great good, and experienced contentment, even elation, when stepping into acts of great evil. Vigorous and intentional application of God's general guidance is the single most important principal in wise decision-making.

WHAT IF WE MAKE A MISTAKE?

Despite great care, we may later think we made a wrong choice. This can lead to anger, depression, and even feelings of anguish and hopelessness. What can we do in these situations?

On the positive side, we remember that making mistakes is part of being human; no one is immune. Errors can help us develop humility, be less judgmental toward others, and increase our personal sense of reliance upon God. They can also make us realize the power of forgiveness, and of Christ's peace that can surpass all external circumstances.

Some commitments aren't absolute. If we realize we are going in the wrong direction, we can turn around! We will not let our pride or fear of what others think keep us from correcting the problem. Nor should we ignore the problem and simply distract ourselves with another activity. Instead, we should pray, seek advice, and find a solution.

If we cannot change course, we remember that God can even make positive use of our mistakes (Romans 8:28). We must not allow an error to cripple our lives. Remember the early background of the Apostle Paul? He bitterly opposed the followers of Christ and even had their leaders executed (Acts 6:8–8:3). When Paul finally recognized the authority of Christ, he turned around completely. Though deeply sorrowful about his past as a persecutor, he did not let it stand in the way of his new life.

We too must remember that Christ forgives us when we fail. In this regard, the words of John Henry Jowett (1863–1923), an influential British pastor, are most encouraging:

> "It is the very gospel of Jesus' grace that He can repair the things that are broken. He can restore the joints of the bruised reed. He can restore the broken heart. He can deal with the broken vow. And if Jesus can do all this, can He not deal with our mistakes? If unknowingly we went astray and took the wrong turn, will not Jesus' infinite love correct our mistakes, and make the crooked straight?"[6]

Indeed, He can transform terrible situations, making them beautiful.

And finally, sometimes it's best not to judge a decision too soon. A good decision does not guarantee an easy path. More often, trouble, unanticipated challenges, and temptation to turn back will arise. But what we initially thought was a disastrous decision may turn out to be best after all.

WHICH CAREER?

I continued growing in my faith throughout high school, especially compelled by the influence of classmates who were ahead of me in their own walk with Christ. I watched with admiration as they handled the challenges and decisions surrounding dating, part-time jobs, future career preparation, and, yes, school athletics.

My cross-country coach was indignant. The school year started, and I did not join his team. "As a senior," he exclaimed, "I expected you to be team captain and for you to be an example for the younger runners!"

"Coach," I appealed, "cross country is just four months, but life is 80 years. I've got to take a time out and make a plan for my game."

First, I prayed for insight. Among my Christ-following friends were several others facing similar decisions. When we met in the mornings before class, we prayed as a group for insight into these decisions.

6 John Henry Joette, *Things That Matter Most* (New York, NY: F.H. Ravell, 1913).

Regarding career choices, my math skills were still poor, music performance had not improved, and business seemed even less of a fit for me. I expanded my options, also considering aviation, politics, and even alternative energy. For each, I listed pros and cons on a grid, taking into account educational requirements, job security, personal interests, salary potential, and the free time each would allow.

Next, I looked in the Bible for advice. I wanted a career that would support my future family (2 Thessalonians 3:10), and I could perform very well (Colossians 3:23–24). But beyond this, I found no instructions about what career to choose. I felt undecided, and the deadlines for college application were looming. What helped at that point was some good advice. I talked with teachers for advice. I even interviewed professional musicians, airline pilots, government officials, and engineers. But what helped most was talking with my parents. They confirmed that none of these were a good career track for me.

Browsing the public library stacks one day, my eyes were mysteriously drawn to a compelling title, *Deliver Us from Evil.* I pulled the book and began leafing through the pages. The author, Tom Dooley, was a United States Navy physician working in Vietnam during the 1950s. A graduate of Notre Dame and St. Louis University, he spoke French, and because Vietnam had been a colony of France, Dooley's language skill was a powerful asset.

At that time, a partition was forming between the communist government of North Vietnam and the government of South Vietnam. As the border hardened, people fled in massive numbers — seas of people who were scared, hungry, sick, injured, cold, and often separated from their parents and families.

Into this mayhem of suffering humanity, Dooley and his corpsman provided food, shelter, medical treatment, and at least briefly, a powerful sense of security and hope while the people were being evacuated. As he worked, Dooley's initial shock over their suffering gradually transformed into deep compassion. He soon recast his initial "society doctor" career plan and invested the remainder of his short life into establishing clinics and training national health workers in Southeast Asia.

I devoured the book. Next, I enthusiastically researched humanitarian relief organizations, refugee care agencies, disaster response groups, and international medicine establishments. This field of work aligned with biblical guidance, the cultural skills I had developed as a teenager in Greece, and even the advice and affirmation of my parents. Forget about designing airplanes, was my enthusiastic conclusion. This is what I want to do!

Deliver Us from Evil, by Dr. Tom Dooley, published by Signet, 1961.

Chapter 6

Treasure Investment Plan

"*My little girl* is so sick! Please, can't you help her?" beseeched a young mother in broken Spanish. "Yesterday, Maria began to vomit. Her fever was unrelenting. Our community health worker was bewildered, so we launched the canoe." Where they arrived was the Clinica Evangelica Morava along the Mosquito Coast of eastern Honduras. I was now a senior medical student on location with my supervisor, Dr. Samuel Marx.

I approached the six-year-old, who was lying on an exam table bathed in sweat. Her eyes were jaundiced and hardly reacted with the normal surprise reaction of seeing a foreigner. I was examining her flaccid arms and legs, when suddenly her entire body tensed up. Maria's head rolled, her back arched and arms and legs begin to slowly convulse, gaining speed and intensity. I flung myself across the little girl to prevent her falling to the floor.

Maria's mother let out a scream, the girl's convulsion intensified, and into this mayhem strolled Dr. Marx. A tall, older gentleman with gray hair, his calmness denoted years of experience. He gently laid his hand on Maria's head, connoting concern, and observed as the spasms of her extremities began to subside. He spoke with her mother in the Miskito language and then turned to me.

"What do you think is causing her febrile illness?" inquired Dr. Marx.

Just prior to arriving for my two months at Clinica Evangelica Morava, I was caring for pediatric patients at Kansas City's Children's Mercy Hospital. Drawing upon that recent experience with febrile kids, I replied, "Maybe an ear infection, otitis media, with a febrile seizure," I suggested.

Dr. Marx looked down, shook his head, and exclaimed, "What of importance do they teach in medical school anymore?" Then he gazed at me. "What did you learn about malaria?"

"Very little," I nervously confessed. "We had one presentation about malaria in microbiology class, but that was three years ago."

Little Maria was waking up now, and her mother let out a long sigh of relief. Dr. Marx shared with her some Miskito language expression of reassurance. Then, taking a cotton ball with alcohol, he wiped Maria's finger, and with a tiny lancet drew a drop of blood which he spread on a microscope slide. I followed him into the laboratory where Dr. Marx smeared the blood into a thin layer, applied Giemsa stain, and analyzed the slide with a light microscope.

"Take a look for yourself," he invited.

I squinted into the lens. "I see normal red blood cells. Oh, but some of them have strange purple rings inside. Could that be malaria parasites?"

"Yes, indeed, Nicholas," ascertained Dr. Marx, "and a patient with malaria plus convulsions is particularly dangerous. That's cerebral malaria, and her risk of death is about one-in-five."

I thought of my own sister, Daphne, just slightly older. What a tragedy to possibly lose Maria! Chloroquine at that time was the treatment of choice. I monitored Maria's progress with her medication, her fluid intake, her fever control.

My purpose, traveling out to work with Dr. Marx, was not simply to experience tropical medicine. Moreover, I came to test the water, to try out for myself the lifestyle of serving some of the most forgotten people in the world; to try out in real time the vision I developed while reading Dr. Tom Dooley's *Deliver Us from Evil.*

With this objective in mind, months earlier I went to Harry Jonas, the dean of my medical school. I did not know any American physician living in a developing nation and doing this kind of work. "Oh, you'll find someone," was Dean Jonas' reassuring reply. "Let me know how it goes." I was successful, but locating a person like Dr. Marx was an arduous experience.

With Dr. Marx's continued guidance, I observed how day by day Maria slowly improved. Day by day, I also experienced growing certainty that, This is indeed what I want to continue doing! And, I realized through my experience caring for Maria that, to do humanitarian work with excellence, I have so much to learn. I'd better make a plan.

Dr. Sam Marx at Ahuas, La Mosquitia, Honduras, on the ham radio — our only communication with the outside world, 1980. Credit: Author's photo.

Nicholas Comninellis at Clinica Evangelica Morava, Ahuas, La Mosquitia, Honduras, 1980. Credit: Author's photo.

PLANNING IS ESSENTIAL

In order to win, sports teams make heavy use of game plans. To succeed, corporations rely upon carefully designed business plans. Governments, schools, and militaries also succeed or fail largely by the plans they develop or fail to develop. To be faithful with the treasure entrusted to us, we too need a plan to help us focus our energy, keep us from becoming distracted, and inspire us when we feel disappointed.

There are a thousand good causes. But if we divide ourselves between them all we will accomplish nothing. Rather, if we focus on one or two, and pursue them with all our resources, perhaps we can prosper. This principle is true in sports, in business, government, academics, even military campaigns. Our mission — the use of our precious treasure — is to love God and people. How much more do we need to plan our own efforts!

God is concerned about our plans. Proverbs 16:3 reminds us to, "Commit to the LORD whatever you do, and he will establish your plans." Building plans upon our commitment to Christ demonstrates the veracity of our faith. James 4:13–17, on the other hand, describes the plight of those who plan without reference to Him, and adds a warning, "… If anyone, then, knows the good they ought to do and doesn't do it, it is sin for them."

GAME PLANNING 101

A plan is a comprehensive statement of the goals we have chosen. Ideally, each goal is the result of careful decision making, vigilant application of the P O P C O R N guidelines.

What do good plans look like? They are:

REALISTIC

We must ask ourselves how much time and energy are demanded, and whether we have the necessary resources. All of us have certain limitations to consider: emotional, physical, financial, and more. Some of us repeatedly fail because we choose formidable tasks with little chance of success. A solution is to select ones that are reasonably attainable. Then, with experience, perhaps create larger undertakings.

SPECIFIC

We do well to aim at clear targets so we will know when we've hit them. Instead of setting a goal to "earn more money" or to "make better grades," we change it to "earn an additional $5000" or "make at least an 'A' average next semester." Rather than making a plan to be more friendly, we identify some particular person to get to know. The best plans are the ones that can be written down, measured, and given a deadline.

FLEXIBLE

Occasionally our situation will shift. A personal, corporate, or national crisis can arise without warning and suddenly force us to alter our intentions. Flexibility means we can continue to fulfill our good intentions despite changed circumstances. The Bible describes two concepts of time. The first is chronos, meaning the days and hours by which we schedule our activities. The second is kairos — referring to events or opportunities that may abruptly appear. Awareness of the kairos is essential, calling us to stay vigilant to the occasions surrounding us.

COMPREHENSIVE

The best plans take into account our important relationships. Many people mistakenly become preoccupied with one aspect of life — often work or romance — and neglect most of the others. A comprehensive plan can be a tool to help us focus attention on everyone who is significant in our network of connections.

PRIORITIES PLEASE

Shauna, one of my University of Missouri Kansas City medical school classmates, was under pressure. It was eight o'clock at night and she still had a presentation to prepare for the hospital seminar the next day. Her books and academic articles were spread out over the table. Shauna was pondering the introduction when her eyes fell upon her calendar. "Oh no!" she sighed, "I promised to help Maria with her Spanish. She'll be here in 30 minutes. I'll just have to work faster!" Shauna concentrated on pulling elements from the documents into her PowerPoint.

Suddenly, Shauna heard pounding on the door. Five of her friends were out front. "We're all going out for pizza!" they called in unison. "Please come with us!"

Now, Shauna was really in a fix. She craved personal interaction with her friends. But there was her presentation, and the Spanish lesson, too. "I'd really like to come," she confessed, "but I'm swamped!"

Like Shauna, we all sometimes feel overwhelmed by all the responsibilities, opportunities, and choices we must make. Elimination is the only alternative. We must decide which are most important, and to focus our energy on these. Only then can we avoid the inevitable fatigue, inefficiency, frustration, and failure that results from attempting too much.

Some followers of Christ try to resolve this tension by ranking their relationships, saying, for example, that Christ always comes first, family always comes second, friends always come third, and so forth. Then, when any conflict comes up, the priorities automatically dictate who will win out.

But this approach raises hard questions. What does it mean to put Christ first? Does it mean we pray four hours a day? Should we do anything that would put Jesus second? Does it mean that when we are at work, Christ is out of the picture and work is now first? If talking with our friends about Christ's message is higher priority than work, should we ever go to work? And, if our personal needs are prioritized in last place, how can we justify eight hours of sleep, two hours of eating, and one hour of grooming each day? If the time we allocate is the measure, then we ourselves are certainly priority number one!

Does a better way exist to approach priorities? In Chapter Five, we looked at Christ's great commandment: "... Love the Lord your God with all your heart and with all your soul and with all your mind." 'This is the first and greatest commandment. And the second is like it: "Love your neighbor as yourself." 'All the Law and the Prophets hang on these two commandments'" (Matthew 22:37–40).

Look closely at this quote. How does Christ position the second command? He says it is like the first one. The word "like," or homoios in the original Greek language, is an important one. It means "similar to this." Christ is indicating that the second command — to love your neighbor as yourself — is also "great and foremost" because it is "like" the first commandment. It is just as important. "Second" in the context of this quote does not indicate second in rank, for the two commands are not being ranked, but listed.

Victor Paul Furnish, in *The Love Command in the New Testament,* explains: "In effect, then, the scribe is being told that no one command can be marked as 'first,' but that these two together... constitute the essence of the law."[1]

1 Victor Paul Furnish, *Love Command in the New Testament* (Nashville, TN: Abingdon Press, 1972).

When we love God, others, and ourselves, there are tremendous overlapping effects, for no relationship is exclusive. J. Grant Howard, professor at both Western Seminary, Portland, and Phoenix Seminary, elaborates on this truth:

> "There are three priorities in life. My responsibility to God, to others, and to myself. They are closely related to each other. Let's make that a stronger statement. They are inextricably tied together.
>
> "When you pray, you are loving God. That's putting God first, but it is also putting yourself first, because you benefit from praying. When you memorize Scripture, you are loving God and in so doing putting Him first. At the same time, you are profiting from the Word and that means you are meeting your own needs, too. When you worship and praise God, He is pleased because of your response to Him. Those very same activities are also having an impact on your personal growth.
>
> "In the same way, when we fulfill a biblical obligation to a neighbor, we put our neighbor first. But the good deed also has numerous positive effects on us. In carrying out our biblical responsibilities to God and neighbors, we are always in some way involved. We are always in some way both contributor and receiver."[2]

When we set priorities, our intention is to be true to each of our important relationships, while staying within the bounds of our time and energy. This is not such a foreign idea. When we live on a budget, we have a certain amount of money to spend on necessities without overdrawing our account. The surest way to deal with conflicting priorities is to choose those which strengthen our important relationships. Other invitations are often simply distractions.

HOW MUCH IS ENOUGH?

Accompanying our sense of responsibility to wisely use our treasure may also be an unhealthy sense of pressure to perform — to earn more, serve more, help more, counsel more, encourage more. The temporary stress of a crisis, of course, can give us lifesaving energy.

2 J. Grant Howard, *Balancing Life's Demands* (Portland, OR: Multnomah Press, 1983).

But the negative effects of long-term pressure are profound: physical illness, depression, poor school or job performance, disturbed family or intimate relationships, and so on.

While in medical school I read the compositions of Richard Swenson. A family physician, he was often literally saving lives and often reaching out to needy people. But Dr. Swenson also felt profound stress and exhaustion. He was living on the edge of burnout.

In a moment of inspiration, Dr. Swenson realized he must take back control over his life. Dr. Swenson painstakingly reexamined all his "good" activities, paying close attention to his own emotional, spiritual, and financial resources. As he cut back his commitments, 90 percent of the psychological pain disappeared. Dr. Swenson also made a startling discovery:

> "With more time on my hands I began to examine the forces that were so chaotically propelling not only my schedule but our culture, too. Where was all the stress coming from? Why was there so much anxiety, frustration, and depression? Why were so many people so unhappy even though they had so much?...
>
> "It was the pathological absence of what I call 'margin' — the gap between rest and exhaustion, the space between breathing freely and suffocating. Margin, the leeway between our reserves and our limits, was missing.... Overload is clearly a common American experience and, naturally, margin is in epidemic short supply. From activity overload to debt overload to work overload, we are a society running on empty. I discovered that the vast majority of people are better off if they draw the line somewhere short of overload, if they preserve some margin."[3]

Just how much treasure-centered activity is enough? If we love God, cherish our family, care for those in our churches, share the Good News with lost friends, do our profession well, and take care of our personal needs — this is an exceptional life. Before setting out to better the rest of the world, we do very well to assure that our private lives are first in order; that we have the resources to match our personal commitments, plus a little extra in reserve.

3 Richard Swenson, "Overcoming Overload," Physician, Focus on the Family, Jan/Feb 1994: p. 20.

WHAT IS YOUR TREASURE INVESTMENT PLAN?

In football, the competition is divided into halves and quarters. This gives the teams a brief chance to rest, reevaluate, and plan for the next period of play. Our lives can also be divided into segments for similar reasons. Parallel with halves and quarters might be school semesters, the time between holidays, or the terms of contracts. In each segment of life, we can form a comprehensive plan that addresses how we will use our treasures in light of each of our relationships.

Useful aids with which to keep your plans organized can include a digital task management app, a smart calendar, or even a simple loose-leaf notebook. First, choose a time segment, such as the next three months. What do you most want to accomplish with your resources during this time period? Record this list in your device. Remember, your intention is not necessarily to do more activities. Rather, it is to engage in the best ones! Your plan might look similar to the following:

Treasure Investment Plan, January to March		
Relating to Christ	Study carefully the Book of John	
Relating to Others	Family:	Help my parents with retirement planning
		Teach my cousin to play guitar
	Christ Followers:	Teach in the youth group
		Make a financial gift to my church
	Lost People:	Talk with Luke about how I became a follower of Christ
		Send a monetary gift to the church plant in Uzbekistan
	Work:	Ace the final exam in Spanish
		Train my new colleague at work
	Relating to yourself:	Jog 2 miles every day
		Sleep at least seven hours each night

Life's responsibilities and opportunities are multiple and interconnected, and none of us can simply concentrate on one sphere alone. For this reason, your plan must address all your important relationships. Combat the temptation to view your plan as confining. Rather, view it as freeing — freeing you to do the best with the resources entrusted to you.

When you reach your deadline, look at your plan and write "Done!" beside each accomplishment. Congratulate yourself. Enjoy that brief timeout between quarters. Then, create a plan for the next segment of time. It might look like this:

Treasure Investment Plan, April to June		
Relating to Christ	Learn about Christ's Second Coming	
	Contemplate actions based on the Book of John	
Relating to Others	Family:	Plan this summer's family reunion
		Take my daughter to visit potential colleges
	Christ Followers:	Take part in the new members meetings at church
		Take part in the new members meetings at church
		Try out for the music team
	Lost People:	Invite Luke to our next church picnic
		Share with Warren my copy of *Mere Christianity*
	Work:	Schedule my summer term
		Develop the new accounting system for the office
	Relating to yourself:	Get my annual medical checkup
		Complete my federal tax return

The segments of time that your plan covers can vary, depending on your needs. You may create a plan for a month, a year, or even five years. Notice how smaller plans can build upon each other to achieve a larger one; like the individual steps that lead us toward the summit of a mountain.

Developing and living by a treasure investment plan may be quite a challenge. Relationship orientation often does not come easy. Extensive planning is often uncomfortable. Relationship-oriented people may resist planning, and planners often overlook relationships. But if we make wise decisions and center our plans around our relationships, we will be much more successful with our treasures.

TO DO HUMANITARIAN WORK WITH EXCELLENCE, I'D BETTER MAKE A PLAN

Returning from Honduras, I was keenly aware of how deficient my skills were in tropical medicine, surgical and obstetrics procedures, international public health initiatives, and basic health leadership. I determined to make a plan to fill in these gaps. First, I went to my academic advisor, a thoughtful physician with no international or low-resource healthcare experience. He pulled an enormous infectious disease textbook from his shelf, handed me the 15-pound volume and said, "Here, read this!"

I leafed through the 2,000 pages which were in a tiny font. "How will I know what's really important?" I questioned him.

"I don't know," he confessed. "Just read it all."

Next, I searched tropical medicine and global health schools. The pros and cons were stark. Liverpool and London were famous, but far away. Harvard and Johns Hopkins were renowned, but prohibitively expensive. Tulane proved to be affordable, but the curriculum was overly focused on parasitology. None were a good fit for me.

I shared this impasse with my mentor in Honduras, Dr. Marx, appealing to his expertise. "Have you considered Walter Reed, the U.S. Army Tropical Medicine School?" he proposed.

No, I was unaware of that option. In fact, I discovered that Walter Reed allocated tuition-free admissions for a few civilians. In the summer of 1987, I was on the campus of the Walter Reed Army Institute of Research in Washington DC, enjoying tutelage from renowned professors and the company of military medicine colleagues from the world over. Nevertheless, I was taking copious notes in my syllabus about how the learning experience could be improved — unaware of how profoundly useful these notes would be in the future.

I also realized that my humanitarian-health-skill-improvement-plan needed to be broader than school alone. I needed experience, too; preferably experience on location with proficient supervisors. The very best advice I received came from Curtis Dixon, an American theological educator living in Angola, southern Africa. He introduced me to Jean Pierre Brechet and Andre Rohner, Swiss physicians for more than 10 years living and working at the Kalukembe Hospital in that nation. Drs. Brechet and Rohner created for me a six-month curriculum, serving under their guidance in the departments of leprosy, tuberculosis, surgery, pediatrics, obstetrics, adult medicine, and community health. I relished this precious opportunity to apply what I learned at Walter Reed day by day as I cared for Angolans, supplemented by advice from my mentors. In fact, to this day those were the happiest months of my entire life.

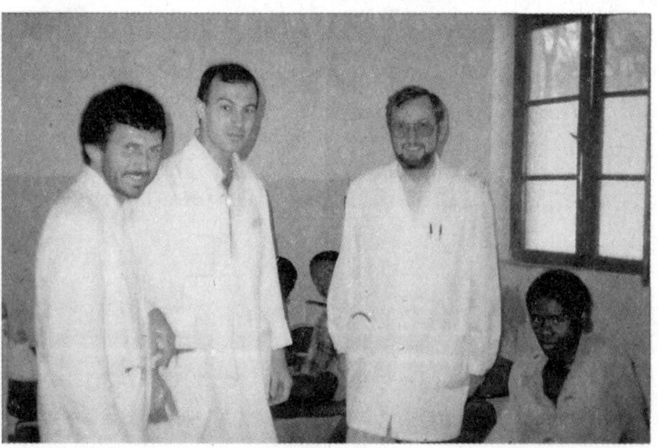

My mentors at Kalukembe Hospital in Angola: Andreas Rohner (left), myself (center), and Jean-Pierre Brechet (right), 1989. Credit: Author's photo.

REAL-WORLD OUTCOMES OF MY SKILL DEVELOPMENT PLAN

One cold evening in Angola, I was summoned to the pediatrics clinic. Isabella, a five-year-old, was in her mother's arms, who gently rocked the girl. Isabella was sweating and listless. Her mother explained that her fever began two days earlier. A community health worker gave Isabella acetaminophen, but fever continued, and the little girl began to vomit.

I examined her eyes. Jaundiced. I inspected her skin. Very pale. I palpated her abdomen. Enlarged liver and spleen. As I turned my attention toward her extremities, Isabella's arms and legs began to shake violently. Her neck arched as the convulsion enveloped her entire body. The mother let out a wail of fear.

A quick injection of diazepam halted Isabella's convulsion. I ran a drop of her blood to the laboratory, confirming under the microscope the presence of malaria parasites. Briefly, my thoughts returned to nine years earlier in Honduras, caring for little Maria — the child with cerebral malaria whom I misdiagnosed. Dr. Marx wisely took advantage of that teachable moment to correct my error and tactfully point out my skill deficiencies.

Minutes later, Isabella was receiving intravenous quinine and glucose, the recommended therapy at that time. By morning, she was fully awake, taking cornmeal porridge spooned by her relieved mother.

Dr. Rohner came by, greeted me with his relentlessly optimistic smile, and spoke in Portuguese with a delightfully German accent. "Cerebral malaria?"

I nodded in the affirmative.

"Oh, very dangerous!" he observed, looking over her intravenous medications. "Nicholas, how did you become so skilled in managing this deadly infection?"

"I participated in several hours of malaria management exercises at Walter Reed. Those were quite insightful," I replied. "In the laboratory, we dissected mosquitoes, extracted the parasites, and tested therapies," I added. "But by far the very best skill development, Dr. Rohner, was actually working together with you month-by-month here in Angola and modeling the expertise with which you care for such patients!"

Chapter 7
Treasure Investment Power

My new city in Angola, Huambo — formerly Nova Lisboa — was situated on a high plateau in the country's interior. Immediately upon arrival, leaders of the churches who invited me were quick to warn that my family and I should be securely inside our home before sunset, with the doors locked and the lights down low. They explained that by day, the city was controlled by one military force. By night, rival soldiers from the other military force made regular advances throughout the city, with battles ensuing between the two. On top of these dangers, gangs of thieves prowled about in the darkness. "Never ever, under any circumstances," exhorted my hosts, "will you open your door at night!"

This all struck me as overly cautious. Weather in the interior of Angola was mild and beautiful, and on the first day I observed people walking freely about on the tattered streets. I felt no necessity to interrupt the pleasant tranquility of staying outdoors. Then suddenly, even before dusk, machine gun fire erupted in the distance, followed by explosions from various directions, smoke billowing into the air.

With haste, I scurried to the house assigned by my hosts. Still missing windows and latches, in the beginning the house promised little security in our first days there. But over the ensuing months I worked to board up the windows, install locks on the doors, and rudimentary alarms on the gates. Most importantly, I assured that my family and I were absolutely indoors long before nightfall.

I had greatly enjoyed the experience of serving at Kalukembe Hospital, especially my collegial interaction with excellent Angolan nurse practitioners. But the hospital's rural location was a mixed blessing.

It provided some protection from the war but was also largely inaccessible to people who had no option but to walk there.

The city of Huambo, by contrast, was home to some 300,000 citizens. Each day I led a small team of Angolan nurses and medical students in providing care via mobile clinics that we held at five different locations, on a schedule of one each day of the week. The medical work in this city was particularly exhausting: caring for unvaccinated children with measles, older adults short of breath from heart failure, malnourished farmers with advancing leprosy, and as many as 100 patients each day suffering from acute malaria infection.

As a young medic, I worked diligently to develop my expertise in medicine and public health. I also strove to master both Mandarin and Portuguese — investing two years respectively in language schools to both understand the cultures and communicate effectively in China and Angola.

My plan moving forward was to care for as many patients as possible. However, under the crushing load of multitudes in need I realized viscerally that many more professionals with similar vision and skill were essential. But who would recruit and equip them?

After one particularly arduous night we were locked inside, when around 11 p.m. a sudden pounding emanated from the front door. The pounding became louder, now like a hammer, rattling the entire metal panel. My preschool children, Elizabeth and James, began crying in fear, and baby Josh wailed uncontrollably. My wife, Teri — who normally was exceptionally comfortable and skilled with all manner of cross-cultural encounters — was alarmed and hurried our children into the basement. I eased to the front window and peered into the yard. A young man in battle fatigues held a rifle with a 30-round ammunition clip, smashing its butt against the entrance to the house. And he was not alone. Twenty more soldiers stood in the yard, peering back at me, weapons in their hands. Parked on the street, a green transport truck with huge tires and more soldiers in the back.

In that moment, I remembered with angst my host's admonishment: "Never ever, under any circumstances, will you open your door at night!"

Glancing out the windows, I confirmed my house was completely encircled. The pounding grew louder still, with the shouts of, "Somos o exército! Abre a porta imediatamente!" That is, "We are the Army. Open the door immediately!"

I felt terrified, exhausted, and conflicted. Certainly, I concluded, these combatants were determined to come inside, and my resistance was futile. So I went to the latch, shoved it to the side, and the door creaked open.

In the Angolan city of Huambo, Pastor Benoliel sternly cautioned me to never open the door of my house at night, 1990. Credit: Author's photo

POWER IN SHORT SUPPLY

Opposition, doubt, and distress predictably afflict anyone who is trying to do good. Such assaults are especially likely when they are least expected, and one is most unprepared.

David Livingstone, immediately upon arrival in present day South Africa, was attacked by a lion whose bite crushed his shoulder, causing paralysis of his right arm, which hung limp by his side for 32 years. But this was only the beginning. During his 10 years as a missionary physician and then 22 years of exploration of the African continent, Livingstone witnessed the summary murder of 300 Africans by slave traders. His food and medical supplies were repeatedly stolen. Livingstone's guides deserted him and falsely reported his demise. His wife went missing and after being found later died of malaria. Livingstone himself suffered from cholera, pneumonia, tropical ulcers, schistosomiasis, and ultimately died of malaria and amoebic dysentery.

Mother Teresa in Calcutta, India, struggled to get permission from the Roman Catholic Church to launch her Missionaries of Charity. Once recognized by the Vatican, local resistance was fierce over her opposition to abortion and contraception, her alleged misuse of financial gifts, as well as over the poor conditions in her homes for disabled street people. Resources for medical care and pain control were often in very short supply. She herself suffered from coronary artery disease, pneumonia, malaria, and heart failure. Most striking, Mother Teresa frequently described crises of faith and feeling abandoned by God.

Scott Armistead, on first arrival to Pakistan in 1999, quickly felt like a failure. His team disbanded because of seemingly insurmountable problems at the hospital and mission. Dr. Armistead and his family left the country for a time to process, pray, and regroup — planning to return to Pakistan the following year. But then 9/11/2001 changed the landscape of Pakistan. Multiple terrorist attacks, including that on a neighboring mission hospital and school, thwarted their return plan, so they rerouted to the Arabian Gulf, serving at Kanad Hospital for a year and a half while waiting for security improvements. Returning to Pakistan in 2003, security remained a concern — sometimes an outright danger. But Armistead continued serving at Bach Christian Hospital, describing how he, "plodded along with a bit more weight on my back, as plans changed, routes were altered, events were cancelled or rescheduled." Then, in 2015 his son developed a bone-origin malignancy, compelling the family to return to the United States for needed treatment.

Like Livingstone, Teresa, and Armistead, we all face resistance, uncertainty, and pain as we seek to steward and manage with excellence our own bags of gold. Many obstacles relate to:

- Mental health: ongoing anxiety, depression, sleep disorders, and unrelenting stress
- Close relationships: discord among couples, children, parents, and friends

- Personal finances: student loans, credit card debt, inflation, limited income, and job security
- Corporate life: workload, conflicts with coworkers, and disagreements with leadership
- Time management: balancing professional work, family life, physical fitness, and hobbies
- Personal health: disabilities, chronic diseases, and age-related challenges

In the face of such barriers, our vision becomes blurry and inner resources depleted. Where can we possibly find the strength to carry on?

POWER FROM CHRIST

When Christ physically departed Earth, He gave us a commission to share His message and mercy with the entire world. But Christ did not stop at this alone. He also reassured us, "… And surely I am with you always, even to the end of the age" (Matthew 28:20). Christ continues to encourage us today through the ongoing presence and work of his Spirit in our lives, reminding us of His ever-present **L I F E:** His Love, Inspiration, Forgiveness, and Eternity. The Apostle Paul later wrote of this wonderful resource: "I pray that out of his glorious riches he may strengthen you with power through his Spirit in your inner being" (Ephesians 3:16). So, when confronted with seemingly insurmountable obstacles, we do well to remind ourselves once more of the security emanating from the presence of Christ within.

Paul certainly is qualified to speak. In his mission to advance the Good News he went hungry, was beaten with rods, pelted with stones, shipwrecked, and assaulted by bandits, all while sustaining the pressure of his concern for the churches. In the light of this experience, he wrote, "But we have this treasure in jars of clay to show that this all-surpassing power is from God and not from us. We are hard pressed on every side, but not crushed; perplexed, but not in despair; persecuted, but not abandoned; struck down, but not destroyed." (2 Corinthians 4:7–9). Paul is explaining that despite us all being "jars of clay" — fragile and imperfect people — we are nevertheless endowed with the presence of Christ, emanating from within and illustrating how His power is displayed through our weaknesses.

POWER FROM OTHERS

In His very last discourse, Christ emphasized once more the importance of being in network with other followers of Him, saying, "A new command I give you: Love one another. As I have loved you, so you must love one another. By this everyone will know that you are my disciples, if you love one another" (John 13:34–35). When we live like this, with rugged commitment to the welfare of our spiritual sisters and brothers, we have access to a tremendous source of strength. When we feel emotionally discouraged, someone can lift us up (Hebrews 10:25). When confronted with a problem, we can jointly find solutions (Acts 6:1–7). When we err, another can gently correct us (James 5:19–20). By living amid such relationships, we can respond to challenges with remarkable energy.

Within the spectrum of human personalities, different people are uplifted in a variety of ways. Identifying your own or someone else's preferred means of encouragement — their love language — can be pivotal. Compliment and express appreciation with kind words for those who thrive on such statements (words of affirmation). Share undistracted time with people who value one-on-one interaction (quality time). Help with tasks or offer practical support for individuals who are receptive (acts of service). Thoughtful presents, regardless of size, can brighten the day of some who feel especially loved in this way (gifts). For select individuals, an embrace, a hug or gentle pat on the back can be inspiring (physical touch).

By living in the midst of community with other followers of Christ, and growing to know one another's personal attributes, we can respond to inevitable challenges with remarkable energy.

POWER FROM PERSONAL COMMITMENTS

We can also find inspiration deep within ourselves by remembering and honoring the substantial promises we have made. Indeed, at times we may fail, and our performance may be poor, but we nevertheless acknowledge our commitments, we regroup, and we press forward on behalf of our children, our spouse, our community of faith, our professional colleagues, and the world as a whole — especially those precious people who struggle with basic human needs.

Each time we keep a promise, we gain not only the confidence of those around us, but we also are more likely to follow through in the future. By keeping commitments, we build integrity that strengthens our relationship with Christ and creates an influential example for others. Repeated faithfulness results in the power to overcome temptations. Moreover, honoring our commitments often cultivates within us sentiments of deeper purpose, inner peace, and even rich joy. Paul describes this experience, writing, "Now this is our boast: Our conscience testifies that we have conducted ourselves in the world, and especially in our relations with you, with integrity and godly sincerity. We have done so, relying not on worldly wisdom but on God's grace" (2 Corinthians 1:12). Even if we seem to have failed, we can still experience deep reassurance in the conviction of striving for what is right, just, and even God-ordained.

POWER INFUSION

Power from Christ, from others, and from personal commitments are often interconnected with one another into a fabric that is stronger than any of these three alone. How can such power be manifested in daily life?

David Livingstone's worldwide influence was in part due to his prolific compositions. These document how in the face of thievery, brutality, betrayal, and death all around, his strength to overcome hardship was grounded in his faith, his sense of mission, and his determination to bring education, medical care, and the Good News into the lives of Africans. "Fear God and work hard,"[1] expresses his conviction that diligence, guided by faith, could conquer such adversity. In particular, Livingstone was committed to abolishing the slave trade, famously declaring, "If a commission by an earthly king is considered a high honor, how can a commission by a heavenly King be regarded as a sacrifice?"

David Livingstone was also deeply encouraged by fellow missionaries, particularly Robert Moffat, who was stationed in South Africa. Additionally, the positive reception of Livingstone's discoveries in Britain, made known through his writings, led to further support for his expeditions and advocacy. Livingstone's sense of divine purpose, along with a genuine love for Africa and its people, compelled him to strengthen his resolve as he built deep relationships among them

1 W. Pakenham Walsh. *Modern Heroes of the Mission Field* (New York, NY: F.H. Revell, 1915).

and advocated for human rights on the international stage. David Livingstone declared, "I am prepared to go anywhere, provided it be forward."[2]

Mother Teresa, a symbol of compassion and unwavering dedication in service to the poorest of the poor, nonetheless confronted incessant denunciation, physical afflictions, and moments of deep spiritual turmoil. How did she endure? Mother Teresa often spoke about how prayer and trust in God sustained her, saying "Prayer is not asking. Prayer is putting oneself in the hands of God, at His disposition, and listening to His voice in the depths of our hearts."[3] Her spiritual discipline of prayer was a lifeline, and even in moments when Mother Teresa felt distant from God, her devotion never seemed to waver. Mother Teresa was encouraged by others through public recognition, including awards like the Nobel Peace Prize, media highlighting the plight of the poor she served, support from religious leaders, and the contributions of volunteers and donors who actively participated in her Missionaries of Charity. Her power also emerged from her genuine compassion for those whom society had cast aside: those homeless, blind, crippled, HIV infected, elderly, unwed mothers, abandoned children, and people terminally ill. Mother Teresa was committed to demonstrate love and dignity toward each one, often saying, "If you can't feed a hundred people, then feed just one."[4]

Scott Armistead diligently explored how to not only survive but thrive amid challenges and adversity. He offers a few pearls forged in the valleys of difficult circumstances: "Adversity is the expected norm and there is no cultural plausibility to the thought that the goodness of God is somehow negated by the existence of suffering in the world. A relational community bears the adversity, finding comfort in one another, in rituals of lament, and, for those who follow Christ, in the sufferings of God Himself and the hope of what is to come. The perspective that virtues emanate from those who undergo

---

2 W. Pakenham Walsh. *Modern Heroes of the Mission Field* (New York, NY: F.H. Revell, 1915).

3 Joseph, Teresa. (2020). St. Mother Teresa: With Her Hand in the Hands of God to the Needy. https://www.researchgate.net/publication/344125750_St_Mother_Teresa_With_Her_Hand_in_the_Hands_of_God_to_the_Needy#fullTextFileContent. Accessed February 7, 2025.

4 Joseph, Teresa. (2020). St. Mother Teresa: With Her Hand in the Hands of God to the Needy. https://www.researchgate.net/publication/344125750_St_Mother_Teresa_With_Her_Hand_in_the_Hands_of_God_to_the_Needy#fullTextFileContent. Accessed February 7, 2025.

trials is central to the teachings of the Scriptures, but, in the midst of cultures that highly value entertainment and amusement, we must ask ourselves if we really deeply value and want to intentionally cultivate these virtues. Lastly is the concept of relational joy — knowing the delight of another's love and delighting in the other — be that person God, a spouse, or a friend. Relational joy gives strength to thrive in adversity."[5]

Like Livingstone, Teresa, and Armistead, while managing our treasures we will continue to face opposition, doubt, and distress. And like them, we too have access to remarkable power as we strive forward.

GOD IS NOT ON A HILL FAR AWAY

As my front door slowly swung open, the full lethality of the outside soldiers came into view. Most had a side arm and grenades, some carried bazookas on their back, and each athletic young man held an AK 47 style rifle. Paralyzed with fear, I envisioned what was next: the militants flooding into my home, looting, burning, and assassinating myself and kidnapping my family.

Seconds past. My palpitations grew stronger, my body now soaked in sweat. "What are they waiting for?" I mused.

A robust older man stepped to the door. He was tall, broad shouldered, dressed in a distinctive uniform with large red lapels on his collars. His deep resonant voice called out to me in Portuguese, "Boa noite. Faz favor, posso entrar?" "Good evening. May I please come in?"

"Ce-ce-certainly," I replied, my voice trembling with each syllable.

The officer strode in, unaccompanied by his entourage. Sizing up the sparse living room, he inquired, "May I have a seat?"

"Ple-ple-please do," was my response, little reassured by his solo entrance.

The general, I surmised from his insignia, settled into a plain wooden chair and seemed to notice the sound of my sobbing children.

"My name is Jobe," he began matter-of-factly, "and these," glancing out front, "are my Special Forces. I hope we have not disturbed you too greatly."

5 Scott Armistead, personal correspondence with Nicholas Comninellis, March 6, 2025.

Seated in an identical chair across from General Jobe, in my apprehension I suffered a language lapse, answering, "我很高兴你来看我. I mean, I'm happy you came to see me," my voice a bit less trembling.

Jobe eyed me thoughtfully, his gaze connoting the care of a grandfather. "Since your arrival in Huambo City 18 months ago, I have closely followed your service to my people, how you have cared for my injured soldiers and treated my neighbor's dysentery. In fact, the infant you managed last week, the one gasping from pneumonia, that was my granddaughter."

Jobe spoke slowly and deliberately, continuing, "But even before I was aware of these kind acts, I was impressed that from a far-off land you would come to share in Angola's troubles."

Jobe paused a moment for emphasis. "I have come tonight to reassure you, Dr. Nicholas, to declare that I am watching over you. My soldiers have been guarding you. You rarely have seen them, but they are protecting you when you go out, as you hold clinics, anywhere you may travel in the city. Fear not!"

I felt stunned, stupefied, suddenly encouraged just when least anticipated. Only then did I notice how Elizabeth, James, and Josh stopped crying. I let out a long sigh.

General Jobe stood to leave. "Angolans," he observed, 'think that God lives on a mountain top far away and thinks nothing at all of us. But this is untrue, Dr. Nicholas. God cares, listens, and already is among us. How do I know? Because of the compassion and service of His people."

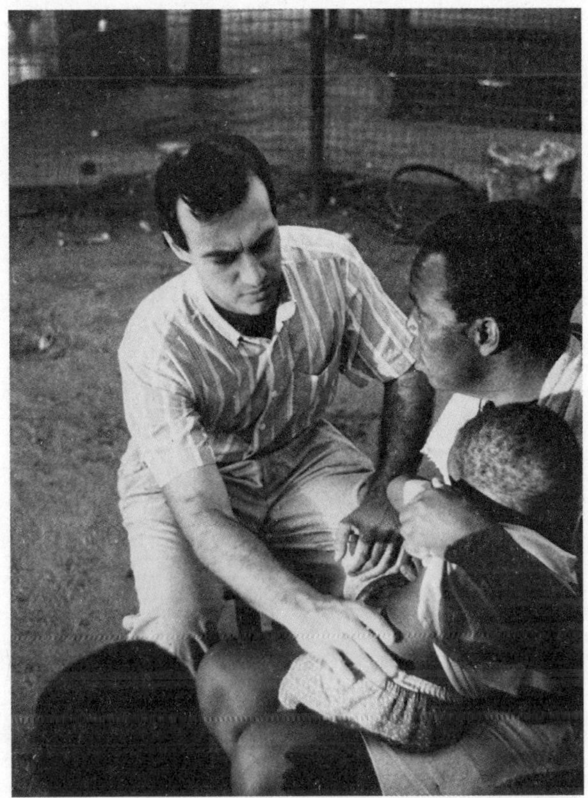

Nicholas Comninellis examines an Angolan child suffering from amoebic dysentery, 1991. Credit: Authors photo.

Chapter 8

Treasure Investment via Spiritual Gifts

Military fighter aircraft now streaked overhead almost every hour. Angolans in the marketplace, normally animated and chatting in groups, began packing up their wares early in the afternoon. As sundown approached, machine gun fire and the boom of cannons broke each evening twilight. Shot-up soldiers, burned children, and maimed families now arrived daily seeking care for their wounds. From my vantage, the war was clearly intensifying.

For five years I had lived outside of the United States. My first two years at Shanghai Charity Hospital were an utter contrast with what followed in Angola. Shanghai was urban and peaceful, and Mandarin was difficult. Angola was agrarian and embattled, and Portuguese I found considerably easier to learn. The throughlines to both peoples were their humble lifestyle and generous spirit. Beyond these, Chinese and Angolans shared little in common. I often wrestled with the logic of investing so heavily in two such contrasting locales.

The desperate plight of Angola's people — those like John the Baptist — weighed heavily on my conscience, and my intention was to stay on location for at least another decade. But then, came the call on the Doctors Without Borders radio....

Communication within Angola circa 1991 was essentially word-of-mouth alone. I was offered a short-wave radio but flatly declined given the accompanying risk of being suspected as a spy. Doctors Without Borders, headquarters a few miles away, accepted that risk, nonetheless. One afternoon they urgently summoned me to their radio.

When I arrived, the Doctors Without Borders staff — mostly Europeans in their 20s and 30s — looked exhausted and worried as they stood around the radio. A scratchy but familiar voice came through from Mission Aviation Fellowship. “Heightened insecurity. Impending strike.” At these words, the European staff all suddenly appeared extremely apprehensive, and I could distinguish that the voice on the radio was trying to choose words that would not raise suspicion among the military minders who were surely listening in. The last phrase from Mission Aviation Fellowship before the staff broke off our transmission was, “Last flight out. Only chance. Tomorrow.”

Just a week later, the rebel army living in the bush launched a bloody and powerful offensive against the government forces within the city, taking over military control, looting and shutting down the hospital, and slaying innumerable civilians. Such armed offensives soon embroiled the entire nation, followed by hunger and starvation that continued for three full years.

I returned to my homeland in the United States, just north of Kansas City, Missouri. Rattled and bewildered, I struggled. The human needs among those who were poor and victims of war were vast, and I enjoyed an extraordinary privilege to serve among them. In the case of Angola alone, thousands of like-minded humanitarians were desperately needed, and now I was out of the mix. This was not my plan. I needed to reset, reassess, and replan. But how?

Nicholas Comninellis guiding Horacio Chipiqito, Angolan medical student,1991. Credit: Author's photo.

SPIRITUAL GIFTS ILLUMINATE A PATHWAY

For a follower of Christ uncertain about future steps, as I was, exploring spiritual gifts can provide much-needed illumination. Upon His physical departure from earth, Christ promised that the presence of His Spirit would reside within us all. Part of this benefit is to empower us with spiritual gifts in order "to equip his people for works of service, so that the body of Christ may be built up" (Ephesians 4:11–12).

What are these spiritual gifts? Romans 12:6–8, 1 Corinthians 12:4–11, and 1 Corinthians 12:28 are the three main sections of the New Testament describing them. Among the spiritual gifts are:

- **Teaching** — Explaining and analyzing biblical truth in a way that clearly informs the hearers.
- **Wisdom** — Understanding biblical truth in such a way as to skillfully apply it to life situations.
- **Leadership** — Guiding other followers of Christ, especially within a church, into deeper faith and stronger works.
- **Encouragement** — Calling on others to follow Christ's truth, especially when confronting trials.
- **Evangelism** — Inviting people who have never begun to trust in Christ.
- **Faith** — Remaining unshakable in our faith despite extreme challenges.
- **Giving** — Sharing joyfully with others from the treasures we possess.
- **Prayer** — Communicating with Christ in a way that fosters intimacy with Him and intercession on behalf of others.
- **Mercy** — Showing compassion to people, especially those who are in distress.
- **Serving** — applying our skills to fulfill the needs of others.

Followers of Christ are each endowed with one or more of these gifts. Clearly there exists some overlap between them. Rather than dwelling upon the exact definitions and delineations, we do better to focus upon the purpose of the spiritual gifts: to facilitate us in symphony to work together to build up our churches, to honor Christ, and to serve others.

What does this look like in action? Consider some examples. The gift of teaching helps to inform biblical truth, enabling Christ's followers to grow in their faith and live according to His commands. The gift of leadership ensures that churches efficiently respond to the needs of those inside and outside. The evangelism gift appeals to those far from Christ to join in following Him, while the gift of mercy demonstrates the compassion of Christ, often throughout the world.

HOW TO DISCOVER YOUR SPIRITUAL GIFTS

The pathway to identifying your gifting can be a fascinating journey. Begin by dwelling upon the above sections within the New Testament that describe this theme. Complement your understanding by taking advantage of excellent books, videos, and webinars on this subject. Within these you will discover structured inventories, that is, surveys that ask questions to probe your particular gifting. These surveys will then produce results that will suggest what may be your spiritual gifts.

Next, talk with your leaders, friends, and colleagues who are also following Christ. Ask them what gifts they may see that are already functioning in your life. This outside perspective may be quite revealing.

Returning to Kansas City, I sought out long-time companions, those who knew me from high school, from college, from my home church, soliciting their sober assessment of my gifts. I was surprised at the results. Long had I considered mercy as my strongest gift. But these confidantes flatly disagreed: no mercy in me. I was perplexed. What were my gifts after all?

One exceptionally effective way to discover your spiritual gifts is to try them out. Like a high school junior athlete selecting from ten different sports, try out for several different teams. Maybe you will excel at wrestling, but you have never competed. Perhaps soccer is your hidden talent, but you have yet to scrimmage.

Similarly, in the context of your church or other ministry, volunteer for a variety of different roles — ones that roughly correspond to the spiritual gifts that resonate with you. Is yours the gift of serving?

Do a stint on the housekeeping team. Could it be giving? Commit for a time to donating more than 10% of your income. Through such experiences you will discover at which roles you excel. Your companions will also subtly observe how well you perform. Putting both together will likely reveal where are you are gifted, and where perhaps you are not.

TREASURE INVESTMENT GUIDED BY SPIRITUAL GIFTS

In the financial world, abundant aids are available to help guide managers to make the most of their money: software tools, wealth advisors, fund administrators, planning calculators. Similarly, in the Christ-focused treasure investment world, powerful aids include POPCORN-based decisions plus identified and tested spiritual gifts.

In applying your gifts, remember that these are designed to be used in synchrony with a body of other Christ-followers, each person adding their special contribution so that the entire group functions far better than individuals could on their own. The Apostle Paul gives us such a picture in 1 Corinthians 12:12, "Just as a body, though one, has many parts, but all its many parts form one body, so it is with Christ."

This variety of gifting encourages healthy interdependence among us all. No single gift is superior to another, and each one is necessary for our churches to function effectively. When each follower of Christ recognizes and appreciates the variety of gifts, it fosters an environment of mutual respect, cooperation, and harmony.

Those with the gifts of teaching, wisdom, and leadership are essential for instructing, mobilizing, and guiding the body. People gifted with encouraging, giving, and serving all strengthen the inner dynamics of the group. Those gifted with evangelism, faith, and mercy are like beacons inviting outsiders to experience the possibilities of trusting Christ.

No more powerful an example of evangelism, faith, and mercy in action can be found than what transpired in Rome during the Antonine Plague (a.d. 165–180) and the Plague of Cyprian (a.d. 249–262). These pandemics, likely from smallpox and measles, killed millions, upending Roman life. Panic and fear led most citizens, including

Roman physicians, to abandon even their own families as they fled the contagion and escaped the city.

In stark contrast, Christians often chose to stay, caring for the sick and dying. They offered medical care, food, compassion, and spiritual comfort to the afflicted, while putting themselves in harm's way, becoming infected, and dying. This radical compassion had profound societal effects, attracting many new followers. Romans saw tangible evidence of the faith's core teachings on genuine love in action. As renowned historian Rodney Stark argues, such acts of mercy played a powerful role in Christianity's rapid growth within the Roman Empire.[1]

Their behavior was not merely humanitarian but also theological and intentional. Early Christian leaders, such as Cyprian of Carthage, preached that suffering was an opportunity to demonstrate Christ's love. They emphasized the importance of viewing all people as neighbors deserving compassion, even in light of personal risk. Dionysius, a bishop of Alexandria, praised Christians who "showed unbounded love and loyalty, never sparing themselves and thinking only of one another. Heedless of danger, they took charge of the sick, attending to their every need and ministering to them in Christ, and with them departed this life serenely happy: for they were infected by their neighbors and cheerfully accepting their pains."[2]

From the extensive historical record, every indication is that Christ profoundly inspired those Romans who claimed allegiance to Him, who then put into action their gifts of evangelism, faith, and mercy. Tertullian, noted Christian leader of that time, observed: "It is our care of the helpless, our practice of loving kindness that brands us in the eyes of many of our opponents. 'Only look,' they say, 'look how they love one another!'"[3]

1 Rodney Stark, *The Rise of Christianity* (San Francisco, CA: HarperSanFrancisco, 1997). P. 86-87.

2 Rodney Stark, *The Rise of Christianity* (San Francisco, CA: HarperSanFrancisco, 1997). P. 82.

3 Tertullian (Latin: Quintus Septimius Florens Tertullianus; c. 155 – c. 220 AD "Apologeticus pro Christianis" (Apology for the Christians). https://www.tertullian.org/articles/mayor_apologeticum/mayor_apologeticum_07translation.htm. Accessed February 2, 2025.

RESET, REASSESS, AND REPLAN

Mercy was apparently not among my gifts. So where was I gifted? I continued to ponder this question as I re-entered life in North America in 1991. The University of Missouri-Kansas City School of Medicine needed faculty to teach family medicine and public health at Kansas City's public hospital. I happily entered that academic world, quite naturally developing syllabi for my learners. Kansas City Cru, Campus Crusade for Christ, desired presentations for students on apologetics. I excitedly developed and delivered such talks covering why we believe what we do. Unparalleled interest in global health was gripping universities throughout the United States, yet these universities had little to offer such students.

Through it all, unrelenting was the burden I continued to sense for those living in low-income communities and nations throughout the world who were needlessly suffering and even dying for lack of basic medical attention. I began imagining an organization that would recruit and equip with excellence those who serve the world's poor via healthcare, one that would also honor and raise the stature of such professionals.

I shared this emerging idea with Roy Moran, primary leader of Shoal Creek Community Church — my homebase in Liberty, Missouri. "Nicholas, you're a natural teacher and thoughtful leader," replied Roy. "This endeavor would be a great match for your gifts." His observation and affirmation were like pressing the ignition switch to a rocket that was ready on the launchpad for liftoff.

First, I pulled the notes I made while studying at Walter Reed Tropical Medicine School. My comments from years earlier about how that learning experience could be improved were suddenly very relevant as I developed my own curriculum surrounding diseases of poverty, maternal newborn care, prevention initiatives, and health leadership for low-resource communities. Throughout, health promotion and community development would be emphasized, realizing that the number of clinicians will never be sufficient to care for so many people in need, and that therefore we must work prospectively to turn off the flood of disease and injury at its source. Furthermore, basic education, literacy, social justice, and economic development would be addressed, since physical health rises and falls with the health of these societal institutions.

I also realized that my students would often be living and working in divergent communities and would need exceptional cross-cultural and even language skills. Soon, the value of my contrasting experience in China and Angola was no longer baffling but providing me precious insights into transferring these abilities.

My students would also need solid, supervised, service-learning experience to apply in real-time when they studied. I recalled as a student myself searching for someone like Dr. Samuel Marx, and how my well-meaning medical school dean had no suggestions. Fortunately, through my experience in China and Angola, I knew several marvelous healthcare professionals. Could they become future preceptors?

As this vision took shape, I also realized it would require enormous time, concentration, and all the leadership and teaching skill with which I was gifted. In this light, I submitted my resignation to the University of Missouri-Kansas City School of Medicine.

One colleague commented, "Wow, you must have received a huge grant to cover your salary while you start this!"

"Not so," I replied. "But the mission is upstanding and syncs well with my strengths."

On June 30, 2003, the first Board of Directors of the INMED — the Institute for International Medicine — gathered around my kitchen table in Liberty, Missouri. Daniel Hickey, Thad May, Roy Moran, Don Philgreen, and I signed on, creating a Missouri non-profit corporation whose mission is to *"Equip healthcare professionals and students to serve the forgotten."*

INMED's founding Board of Directors, left to right: Don Philgreen, Daniel Hickey, Nicholas Comninellis, Micah Flint (first CEO), Roy Moran, and Thad May, 2005. Credit: Author's photo.

Chapter 9
Treasure Investment via Role Models

"*When I was* training to become an eye doctor, we had many successes. These dear people came one after another for eye surgery and the next day were going home rejoicing, able to see again after so many years. People telling me 'Oh this is the first time I have ever seen my little baby's face. She's now three years old!' The tears streaming down her face. Melted my heart!" Steve Collins spoke with passion, with tears in his eyes at his clinic at CEML, Evangelical Medical Center of Lubango in Angola.

"Well, we had one lady come in who had cataracts," continued Dr. Collins, "and I assured her that we would do her procedure and the next day she could go home likely seeing much better than she had been able to for many years. Well, I operated on her. Next day, I went to take her bandage off and I waited for her exclamation of joy and hallelujah over their sight being restored. But nothing! I asked, 'Can you see my hand?'"

"No, Doctor," the elder woman replied matter-of-factly.

"What?" he questioned, exasperated. "I looked at my notes. Seemed to me the procedure went fine."

"No doctor, I can't see," she reaffirmed.

"So, I called in the nurses, 'Did you put the drops in like I told you?' 'Yes, yes,' they replied. "Well, put the patch back on and we'll examine her again tomorrow," recounted Dr. Collins. "I thought maybe it was just some little thing and the next day she could see fine. But next day, same story."

"'No, doctor, I still can't see."

"I started to rail at those who had been on duty overnight. Maybe

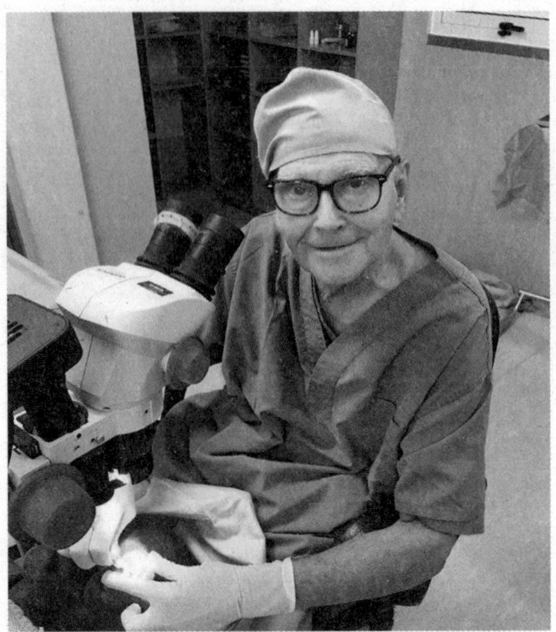

Steve Collin, age 77, performing cataract surgery at CEML Hospital, Angola, 2014. Credit: Author's photo.

they had not given the right medication or fitted her eyepatch properly. I could not conceive of a good reason why she could not see! She reached out and caught hold of my hand."

"Doctor, why are you so upset?" the blind woman exclaimed.

"I said, 'Well, I did an operation on you that was supposed to bring you sight! It hasn't worked. This is tearing me apart!" cried out Dr. Collins.

"Doctor," she replied in a reassuring tone, "Look, I've been blind for nine years, and four years ago, I met someone whose hand I hold every day. He leads me, He's my light. He is enough, his name is Christ. Do you know him?"

"Well, that put me flat to the ground!" proclaimed Dr. Collins. "I was the missionary being taught by one of my patients. She turned out to have optic atrophy, unable to see ever again. In my stage of training, I was unable to recognize preoperatively what might've been the problem. More importantly, I learned that amid all the patients we care for, many we cannot save. Many will die and many will lose their sight. Through it all, we must remember to point them to the

One who is the life. In this light, my failure in caring for this poor woman became one of my greatest successes of all."

Steve Collins, over a 30-year period of living and serving in Angola, restored sight for some 30,000 people. With support from Christian Blind Mission and Mission Aviation Fellowship Canada, he traveled for weeks at a time throughout the most impoverished, neglected eastern cities of the nation. But Dr. Collins was becoming elderly, and while still spry in spirit, he tired more easily. Who would carry on his inspiring service to humanity?

POWER OF EXEMPLARY ROLE MODELS

With the launch of INMED in 2003, I pondered, What will be the most important education methods for INMED learners? Now was my opportunity to make good on the improvements I envisioned while myself in medical school, public health school, and tropical medicine school. Didactic study, certainly important. Hands-on skills, definitely relevant. Simulation exercises, surely valuable. By far the most crucial element, I concluded, is service–learning guided by exemplary role models. I benefited immeasurably from such supervised experience with Dr. Marx in Honduras and Dr. Rohner in Angola. Now, how could I make the case to my board of directors, faculty, and learners of this priority?

BIBLICAL ROLE MODELS AND LEARNERS

As we consider biblical role models and their apprentices, who comes to mind? Perhaps great prophets of old — Elijah, for example, calling Elisha away from plowing fields to learn the ways of a spokesperson for God, or Joshua son of Nun serving as close aide and attendant to Moses, who was preparing Joshua to eventually succeed him after Moses' death as the leader of the Israelites.

The Apostle Paul was also a powerful influencer. After his conversion, Paul focused on making Christ known and establishing churches in regions where there were none. Doubtless, he impacted thousands of people through his personal presence, teaching, and writing. But there was one individual with whom Paul had a very powerful relationship, one documented in the Book of Acts chapters 16 through 18. Paul writes to him in 2 Timothy 3:10–11, "You, however, know all about my teaching, my way of life, my purpose, faith, patience, love, endurance, persecutions, sufferings — what kinds of things happened to me in Antioch, Iconium, and Lystra, the persecutions I endured. Yet the Lord rescued me from all of them."

In this letter, Paul emphasizes the fact that Timothy has not simply heard Paul speak or followed his writings, but that Timothy had actually witnessed the pain and sufferings that Paul experienced in these cities where he was opposed, attacked, and outcast. With this backdrop, Paul nevertheless commissions Timothy to "preach the word; be prepared in season and out of season; correct, rebuke and encourage — with great patience and careful instruction" (2 Timothy 4:2). In essence, Paul was urging Timothy to announce the Good News, whether or not the situation was comfortable, whether or not he felt prepared, and then to apply the teachings of Christ to everyday situations while employing restraint and skilled coaching.

How did Timothy act upon the commission received from Paul? Timothy pastored the church in the city of Ephesus after Paul left for Rome in about a.d. 64. He co-authored several letters that make up the New Testament, including 2 Corinthians, Philippians, Colossians, 1 and 2 Thessalonians, and Philemon. Later, while Paul was in prison, Timothy represented Paul to the churches and brought their news to him behind bars.

BARNABAS AND PAUL

A less recognized but equally powerful example of role modeling is the relationship of Barnabas and Paul. Barnabas first appears in the New Testament in Acts chapter 4: "… From time to time those who owned land or houses sold them, brought the money from the sales and put it at the apostles' feet, and it was distributed to anyone who had need. Joseph, a Levite from Cyprus, whom the apostles called Barnabas (which means son of encouragement), sold a field he owned and brought the money and put it at the apostles' feet."

Here we see Barnabas giving up his personal possessions, surrendering his authority and his wealth to the leadership of the Apostles. Through such actions, we gain perspective into his life. We see Barnabas' qualities of faith in action. Now, move forward to Acts chapter 9 and read what happens next in the life of Barnabas and the early church. Saul, a Jewish zealot, was rabidly pursuing, apprehending, and imprisoning followers of Christ. In an extraordinary display of power, Christ appeared to Saul while on the road to the city of Damascus. Saul experienced a dramatic conversion and immediately began to proclaim in the synagogues that Christ is the Son of God. "All those who heard him were astonished and asked, 'Isn't he the man who raised havoc in Jerusalem among those who call on this name? And hasn't he come here to take them as prisoners to the chief priests?' Yet Saul grew more and more powerful and baffled the Jews living in Damascus by proving that Jesus is the Messiah" (Acts 9:21–22).

Next, when Saul, whose name soon changed to Paul, came to Jerusalem, he tried to join the disciples. "But they were all afraid of him, not believing that he really was a disciple. But Barnabas took him and brought him to the apostles. He told them how Saul on his journey had seen the Lord and that the Lord had spoken to him, and how in Damascus he had preached fearlessly in the name of Jesus. So, Saul stayed with them and moved about freely in Jerusalem, speaking boldly in the name of the Lord" (Acts 9:26–29).

What was the role of Barnabas in Paul's life at this critical juncture? Paul was recently commissioned by God, yet the followers of Christ would have nothing to do with him and, humanly speaking, we can certainly understand their apprehension. How could they trust this man, especially given the way he had persecuted the church? Perhaps his claimed conversion was simply a ploy to infiltrate the churches and later arrest them. But Barnabas, recognizing the genuine spiritual transformation within Paul, took a great risk to his own reputation and brought him before the leaders of the church in Jerusalem, to the Apostles. Barnabas "told them how Saul on his journey had seen the Lord and that the Lord had spoken to him, and how in Damascus he had preached fearlessly in the name of Jesus" (Acts 9:27).

Barnabas, a man of confidence within the leadership of the church, in essence declared, "This is a trustworthy man!" As a result of Barnabas' endorsement, Paul was accepted by the leadership, and with this vote of confidence, Paul stayed among them, "speaking boldly in the name of the Lord" (Acts 9:28).

Barnabas' role was central to launching the ministry of Paul. But this was only the beginning of their collaboration. In Acts 11, we read, "Then Barnabas went to Tarsus to look for Saul, and when he found him, he brought him to Antioch. So for a whole year Barnabas and Saul met with the church and taught great numbers of people. The disciples were called Christians first at Antioch" (Acts 11:25–26).

In the life of Paul, the godly character of Barnabas was surely inspirational. Moreover, Paul's new life in Christ was affirmed by Barnabas and the first steps in Paul's ministry were facilitated by him as well. Humanly speaking, what kind of man would Paul become and how great would his influence be without the role of Barnabas?

CHARACTERISTICS OF EXEMPLARY ROLE MODELS

Beyond biblical examples, role models — especially positive ones — throughout history have been decisive in shaping individuals, societies, and even entire civilizations. From great leaders and pioneering scientists to compassionate educators and tireless activists, exemplary role models inspire us to push our limits, strive for excellence, and contribute meaningfully to our communities. Their influence extends beyond mere admiration; they guide values, aspirations, and behaviors of their apprentices.

Exemplary role models typically possess several characteristics in common:

- **Integrity** — They demonstrate honesty, strong moral principles, and consistency between their words and actions.
- **Perseverance** — They show resilience in the face of obstacles and setbacks, proceeding with determination.
- **Empathy and Compassion** — They understand and care for others, often advocating on their behalf.
- **Dedication to Excellence** — They continuously strive to better themselves and encourage others to strive for quality.
- **Inspiration and Leadership** — They motivate others toward achieving their full potential.
- **Humility** — They intentionally divert attention away from themselves, complementing and crediting their colleagues.

Beyond these virtues, such individuals make themselves available — often quite intentionally — to influence the personal growth of other people. This availability is not without cost, however. The role model may feel that she or he simply does not have time, energy, or capacity to invest into another. And yet, these same individuals recognize that they must invest.

Why? Because observing and learning from a role model often instills into other people the motivation and discipline necessary to pursue a worthy dream. A child who looks up to a teacher who is passionate about learning may develop a plan for further education. An athlete inspired by a sports hero's work ethic may cultivate habits of lifelong fitness. A student, upon hearing the foreign language spoken with excellence, may determine that it can indeed be mastered after all.

More than skill acquisition, role models also help shape the character and values that saturate the entire human experience of those who surround them. When individuals see their role models practicing kindness, humility, or perseverance, they themselves are more likely to integrate these traits into their own lives. This is particularly powerful in formative years when individuals are developing their own worldview and moral compass.

Representation can matter significantly. Seeing a successful role model who shares similar backgrounds, challenges, or aspirations as their observers can be profoundly inspiring. It reassures them that success is attainable, regardless of one's starting point. This is particularly important for observers who originate from minority or marginalized communities, where role models provide hope and a roadmap for overcoming broad barriers.

I never considered myself suppressed by any systemic obstacles. Born and raised in Parkville, Missouri, a small town northwest of Kansas City, mine was a childhood filled with exploring the woods, building dams on the creek, and playing baseball with my friends. Years later, I spoke with one of my Parkville elementary school friends, who exclaimed, "I am so inspired to see how you, from a very modest-income family in our shabby little town, rose to become so successful. This makes me think I could enjoy an awesome life, too." I was shocked at her statement. I never thought much about my family's economic status or the reputation of our hometown. But apparently my later successes helped fuel her own vision of what could be.

WHERE TO MEET EXEMPLARY ROLE MODELS?

In our digital age, technology plays a crucial role. Social media platforms, news sites, and streaming entertainment have the power to amplify positive role models, allowing people to learn from successful figures. But such technology can also powerfully promote individuals who may not exhibit exemplary qualities. The rise of influencers who prioritize fame and followers over virtuous values sometimes leads to the glorification of materialism, superficiality, and even destructive behaviors. Considering these circumstances, each person must even more critically evaluate whom they choose to emulate. Parents, educators, and mentors — you can play an especially crucial role in guiding younger people to identify role models who embody genuine integrity, hard work, and compassion.

Intentionally move beyond the online space and seek out face-to-face interaction. The opportunity to observe those individuals up close, interact with their personal lives, and even participate in activities together is exponentially more powerful than following some media personalities from a great distance.

But where to search within one's physical space? More specifically, Where can I find someone who has the qualities and who is already doing what I dream to do? Begin within your personal networks. Among those in your family, school, profession, church, social clubs, and network of friends, who is such a person or who knows of such a person? Often, within these circles such a role model can be identified.

Beyond personal networks, ask yourself where such a role model would more likely be found. Seminars, workshops, big conferences, schools, universities, or courses that focus on your particular interests will be likely to attract people who may possess the qualities and experience you seek. Finally, by simply engaging in steps toward your vision, you are more likely to encounter and even attract those who share your vision. Among these people you may be impressed to discover attributes you wish to imitate.

EXEMPLARY ROLE MODELS: FOLLOW ONE. BECOME ONE. INSPIRE ANOTHER ONE

The power and importance of exemplary role models cannot be overstated. For we who honestly ponder how to use our treasure, looking up to those who are already faithfully investing the resources bestowed to them cannot only inspire us but provide concrete examples that we ourselves can follow. In summary:

FOLLOW ONE

Exemplary role models can profoundly fuel our values, aspirations, and actual activities — proving that what initially appeared to be a distant virtue is actually achievable in real life. But we must exert some intentional effort to search them out, create a relationship, and take advantage of opportunities to absorb their guidance. For me, the vision created by reading the book *Deliver Us From Evil* was embodied in the life of Dr. Sam Marx, with whom I worked every day for two months as his student in Honduras. Years later, his words, his patient behavior, and his unwavering vision of ministering to humanity continue to inspire me.

Warning: Imperfections will appear. The most model human being also possesses flaws and failures. In fact, if these are not yet apparent, then we likely are not yet familiar with the person. Observing our role model responding positively to their own personal failures can be one of the strongest testaments to that person's character.

BECOME ONE

We each possess the privilege to not only seek out exemplary role models but also to develop and eventually embody within ourselves those values and activities we highly regard. As we continue living in this way, we come to understand the nuances and modalities of excellence that can only be developed through personal experience. In my life, the five years of service at Shanghai Charity Hospital and in the nation of Angola was a precious opportunity to live out that vision day by day, and in the full context of accompanying struggles, doubts, joys, and victories.

A word of caution: Becoming a worthy role model requires more than simply expertise and devotion to a cause. It also requires a vigorously maintained, wholesome personal life. Our finances, our personal relationships, our health habits, our spiritual devotion all must be managed with excellence. Otherwise, how quickly our impact can be destroyed!

INSPIRE ANOTHER ONE

Leaders in positions of influence may not be mindful of their broad impact. When they engage in malfeasance, others will normalize and imitate such behavior. By contrast, when leaders prioritize integrity and responsibility, they can create a culture that encourages observers to follow uprightness. By doing so, leaders contribute to a cycle of initial inspiration, action, and broader influence that propels the vision forward. With the launch of INMED, my colleagues and I quite deliberately set out to highlight the immense value of compassionate healthcare and to create accessible pathways for those inspired to pursue careers of service toward the world's most forgotten.

Obstacles ahead: You who wish to inspire another individual will find that you do not have enough time. Make time anyway. You will discover your energy is insufficient. Press forward, nevertheless. You will question whether your impact is effective. Continue impacting all the same.

INSPIRE ANOTHER ONE: INMED'S EARLY PROGRESS

INMED's first years, 2003–2005, were focused on arranging service-learning experience for medical students, physician assistant students, and resident physicians with carefully selected preceptors — themselves all exemplary role models: Steve Foster living in Angola, Peter Burgos in China, George Faile in Ghana, Dr. Lopez and Dr. Laredo in Honduras, and Lorna Sarra in Zambia.

Emily Schwartz is a strong example of those early INMED learners. A physician assistant student at Philadelphia University, in June 2005, she traveled into the outback of Zambia in southern Africa to serve alongside Lorna Sarra at Mushili Health Center. Reported Emily thereafter, "Being with the others at the mission, experiencing healthcare in another country, this greatly impacted my life. I think the most valuable aspect was seeing the challenges that healthcare providers in Zambia face, with the lack of resources, language barriers, and lack of health education on the part of the communities. My goal was to learn how healthcare systems operate in a third-world country and begin to learn what needs to be done to make the operations better. I believe that I did begin this process, thanks to INMED. I would tell anyone who was interested in international health or an overseas elective that they should do it through INMED. I've come to love Zambia, and I hope God will bring me back."

Quickly we realized that our preceptors expected INMED learners to arrive much better prepared, similar to Dr. Sam Marx's 1981 critique of my deficient knowledge about malaria when I first arrived in Honduras. Our response in 2009 was to launch the INMED Graduate Certificate in International Health — an eight-week course utilizing simulation, role-play, case studies, critical analysis, and small group education techniques to enhance students' ability to apply their skills once on location with their preceptors. This 10-credit hour course embodied many subjects in common with mainstream topical medicine and public health schools, but with an accelerated format and much lower tuition. With expert guidance from INMED's early leaders — Micah Flint, Skylar Rolf, and Elizabeth Burgos — the INMED Graduate Certificate in International Health grew to become INMED's most popular academic offering, with 1,500 total graduates by 2025.

INMED Officers, 2011: Micah Flint (left), Skylar Rolf (center), Elizabeth Burgos (right), Nicholas Comninellis (seated). Credit: INMED.

We also discovered that INMED learners often were lacking in basic clinical skills, a phenomenon unfortunately common throughout health professions schools today. So INMED began offering in-person, hands-on skills training in newborn resuscitation, basic newborn care, maternal care and complicated obstetrics, obstetrics ultrasound, ultrasound for primary care, and wound care plus fracture management — all skills available from specialists in high-resources healthcare settings, but ones in which almost every healthcare professional must be adept to work in low-resource settings.

"Where can I meet others who share an altruistic healthcare vision?" became a frequent question among INMED learners, preceptors, donors, and service establishments. To create such a forum, in 2006 we established the annual Humanitarian Health Conference around the theme Equip, Connect, Go! At this event, participants equip themselves with life-saving skills, connect with like-hearted colleagues and classmates, and arrange to go with esteemed organizations serving the world. James Fyffe, a U.S.-based emergency department nurse, was one such participant. "At the Humanitarian Health Conference I met influential staff from Bach Christian Hospital in Pakistan. They invited me to come visit, and soon I was on location with them in the mountains." A few months later with his wife Rosie and their boys, the James Fyffe family took the next bold step, moving their family to those mountains where James taught for four years at the Bach Christian Hospital school for national nurses. Observed Fyffe, "A little compassion goes a long way, like a light illuminating a dark hill. It's not just about the people whom you touch directly, but also those who become inspired by your example."

"We want to be even better prepared!" was a growing appeal from INMED graduates throughout the 2010s. The idea of offering an INMED master's degree came into view. But with our faculty and staff fully occupied with teaching, precepting, and logistics, where would we find capacity? Then struck the COVID-19 pandemic, shuttering classroom teaching and grounding travel. Suddenly, we had capacity to design the MIH — the Master's Degree in International Health. Building upon the INMED Graduate Certificate Course and well-established INMED service-learning, the MIH added epidemiology, elective courses, and a scholarly project. I was frequently asked, "What is unique about the MIH?" to which I replied, "Our laser focus is on serving forgotten people. This degree is especially for you who are concerned over healthcare for those who are poor, undereducated, minorities, disabled, elderly, veterans, refugees, migrants, chronically ill, and victims of war or disaster. The MIH degree addresses the gaps in traditional healthcare education so we are better equipped to serve these precious people with excellence."

INSPIRE ANOTHER ONE: AN INMED STORY

John Kakorio was one such concerned professional. A physician from Zambia, a nation in southern Africa, John in 2022 wrote to INMED on his MIH application, "Doctors need to understand that the profession is not about the money nor the prestige, but actually about the care of the sick. I want to be part of this type of foundation." John advanced quickly through his MIH academic courses, expressing throughout his special interest in sight preservation, and which culminated in a scholarly project titled Prevention of Blindness in Africa. Next, John needed to complete his MIH supervised service-learning. But with whom? What preceptor could possibly guide John through the practical development of his skills in eye care?

Steve Collins, still in Angola restoring sight for thousands of people each year, was animated at the prospect of John Kakorio working under his tutelage. Together they traveled for weeks at a time throughout the most impoverished, neglected eastern regions of the nation. For more advanced interventions, the two worked together at Boa Vista Eye Hospital on the coast and at Evangelical Medical Center of Lubango on the western plateau.

By now, however, Dr. Collins was becoming even more frail. Who would carry on his inspiring service to humanity? Almost simultaneously, John Kakorio graduated with his Master's Degree in International Health and joined the professional staff of Boa Vista Eye Hospital. Of John Kakorio, Steve Collins wrote shortly before his death at age 85, "Highly enthusiastic. Very hard working. A pleasure to know."

Dr. Kakorio today continues the exemplary work of his role model, caring for those like this 64-year-old man from the town of Cavango, Angola. "He began losing his sight in the 1990s. One of his eyes was operated on in 2000 but the surgery did not go well," detailed Dr. Kakorio. "He was blind all this while until 2024 when Dr Tim

Kubacki from Cavango sent him to me. I examined him and noticed how complicated his case was," described Dr. Kakorio with a shudder. "The man was accompanied by his wife whom he last saw in 2001 and his children whom he had never seen before. The day before his surgery, I prayed about his case, and asked God to give him sight again so that he could see his children, even if it was just for a minute because that's what he really wanted."

"The day following, I couldn't believe the miracles of God when I removed the eyepatch," exclaimed John Kakorio. "His smile, his words, his reaction after seeing his children for the very first time touched my heart so deeply. He couldn't believe that one day he was ever going to see again. Professor, not every case is so successful, but I rejoice with each victory and keep going forward."[1]

Just after removing the eyepatch, he can see for the first time in 25 years! Dr. John de Costa Kakorio and his previously blind patient. Boa Vista House of Health, Benguela, Angola, 2023. Credit: John de Costa Kakorio.

1 John de Costa Kakorio. Personal correspondence with Nicholas Comninellis, December 24, 2024.

Chapter 10
Treasure in Heaven

Life in China in the 1990s was exciting. Economic progress was touching many people. Education opportunities were abundant. Access to electricity, Internet, drinking water, and plentiful food became almost ubiquitous. Availability of specialty medical care mushroomed in the cities. In comparison to what I witnessed in Shanghai a decade earlier, the nationwide transformation was miraculous.

Of special interest to me were two remaining gaps: low-income citizens without medical insurance and the lack of primary medical care professionals to serve such citizens. Cost of medical care in China was low by international standards, but for minimum wage earners even those small fees made medical care prohibitive. When people could afford a medical consultation, it was most often with a sub-specialist physician who was unprepared to address their broad and ongoing health needs. The gaps concerned not only me but also a growing chorus of Chinese leaders.

Into this space stepped Peter Burgos. A physician graduate of In His Image Family Medicine Residency in Tulsa, Oklahoma, Peter spoke Mandarin quite fluently. In 2003, together with a coalition of Chinese healthcare professionals, LIGHT — Liaoning International General Heath Trainers — began preparing family physicians via a three-year program based in Shenyang, a city in northeast China near the border with North Korea. LIGHT's approach was distinctive. Until that time, China had developed few advanced training opportunities in family medicine or other fields of primary care like pediatrics or internal medicine. Peter and his Chinese colleagues were animated as they equipped their graduates to provide comprehensive care for women in pregnancy and labor, newborn babies, children and adolescents, adults, and for the elderly. Such broad skills were ideal for serving communities with few healthcare professionals.

LIGHT's service population was also distinctive. In partnership with local government leaders, LIGHT intentionally sought out opportunities to serve low-income and no-income patients: elderly living in humble nursing homes, special needs children in daycare and orphanages, rural agricultural workers in community centers, as well as students and unemployed residents of the urban landscape. LIGHT's approach was refreshing and holistic. They included physical and occupational therapists, social workers, and special education instructors, all while addressing the comprehensive physical, emotional, and spiritual needs of patients.

In 2011, I began teaching at LIGHT, overjoyed to once again be closely engaged with China and reactivating Mandarin skills with the help of my physician-tutor, Jackie Tong. Soon thereafter, INMED started offering the Graduate Certificate in International Medicine and Public Health at LIGHT's academic center within the H'Image Doctor Clinic in Shenyang. Participating were Chinese physicians and nurses, plus medical students from Africa and southern Asia. These new INMED graduates included a very bright young Chinese physician, Jason Pang. He was not only a keen academic, but also sincerely focused on innovations to aid China's most forgotten people.

Among these forgotten were Chinese living with HIV infection. While they were protected from firing by government rules, coworkers and supervisors would put pressure on these people to leave. If family got word of an HIV-infected relative, that person would predictably often be cut off. So, HIV-positive people usually chose to hide their illness from others.

Those with HIV infection often encountered difficulties in the medical care system. Some staff, especially at smaller hospitals, felt hesitant or fearful about providing care for these patients. Once laboratory results indicated an HIV-positive person, other patients and medical staff would be alerted. Moreover, when a patient tested positive for HIV, the hospital was required to report the case to the local Center for Diseases Control, which could be a complicated and stressful process. So usually, HIV patients tried to hide their medical history.

In this context, a looming question prevailed. Who would readily make available basic primary medical care for people with HIV living largely in isolation?

INMED Graduate Certificate in International Health graduates, Beijing, China, 2019. Credit: Author's photo.

WHAT ACCOUNT WILL YOU GIVE FOR USE OF YOUR TREASURE?

When Christ physically departed earth, He stated quite clearly that He would return again and that a new heaven and new earth would replace the reality that exists today. During this period there will be a special event, the Final Judgement, forecast several times in the biblical narrative, including Daniel 7:9–10, Revelation 20:11–15, and Matthew 25:31–46. The latter record is especially relevant and bears reviewing once again:

> "When the Son of Man comes in his glory, and all the angels with him, he will sit on his glorious throne. All the nations will be gathered before him, and he will separate the people one from another as a shepherd separates the sheep from the goats. He will put the sheep on his right and the goats on his left.
>
> "Then the King will say to those on his right, 'Come, you who are blessed by my Father; take your inheritance, the kingdom prepared for you since the creation of the world. For I was hungry and you gave me something to eat, I was

thirsty and you gave me something to drink, I was a stranger and you invited me in, I needed clothes and you clothed me, I was sick and you looked after me, I was in prison and you came to visit me.'

"Then the righteous will answer him, 'Lord, when did we see you hungry and feed you, or thirsty and give you something to drink? When did we see you a stranger and invite you in, or needing clothes and clothe you? When did we see you sick or in prison and go to visit you?'

"The King will reply, 'Truly I tell you, whatever you did for one of the least of these brothers and sisters of mine, you did for me.'

"Then he will say to those on his left, 'Depart from me, you who are cursed, into the eternal fire prepared for the devil and his angels. For I was hungry and you gave me nothing to eat, I was thirsty and you gave me nothing to drink, I was a stranger and you did not invite me in, I needed clothes and you did not clothe me, I was sick and in prison and you did not look after me.'

"They also will answer, 'Lord, when did we see you hungry or thirsty or a stranger or needing clothes or sick or in prison, and did not help you?'

"He will reply, 'Truly I tell you, whatever you did not do for one of the least of these, you did not do for me.'

"Then they will go away to eternal punishment, but the righteous to eternal life" (Matthew 25:31–46).

Consider the immense resources invested into Adolf Hitler's invasion of Europe, Timothy McVeigh's creation of the explosives used in Oklahoma City, and Bashar al-Assad's weapons for slaughtering the innocents within Syria. What if such commitment and energy were instead directed toward the welfare of these humans? What if instead of being identified as a goat and separated by Christ, such perpetrators directed their innovation and energy toward genuine good toward one another, and were ultimately invited to join Christ's sheep?

The Parable of the Sheep and Goats is a powerful appeal for active faith, faith that results in compassionate service. It challenges us to see Christ Himself in those who are needy and to embody the virtues of love and justice as we defend and empower such people. It also confirms how contrary is the strongman approach to greatness from greatness in the sight of Christ. Ultimately, this parable affirms that genuine faith in Christ is not merely intellectual agreement, but faith that is lived out via our intervention on behalf of humanity.

The Apostle Paul's letter to the Ephesians further illuminates this truth:

> [8]For it is by grace you have been saved, through faith — and this is not from yourselves, it is the gift of God — [9]not by works, so that no one can boast. [10]For we are God's handiwork, created in Christ Jesus to do good works, which God prepared in advance for us to do (Ephesians 2:8–10).

These three verses succinctly capture profound truths about salvation through faith and the relationship between our faith and our actions. Verse 8 emphasizes that salvation — the forgiveness of all trespasses — is a gift from God, freely given and received through faith. The phrase "this is not from yourselves" emphasizes the impossibility of earning salvation via our effort or works.

Verse 9 continues this theme by clarifying that salvation does not result from our undertakings, thus eliminating any grounds for crediting ourselves. It reinforces the idea that faith is humble dependence on God's free gift, rather than some kind of reward for moral achievement. By removing human deeds, Paul emphasizes that God alone deserves credit for spiritual new life we receive.

Next, verse 10 shifts focus to our new purpose in life. Those who are saved — we who are forgiven of all trespasses — are described as God's workmanship, indicating we are intentionally crafted by God. The phrase "created in Christ Jesus for good works" highlights our new purpose for existing and that this purpose "prepared beforehand" is part of God's master plan for humankind.

In sum, these three pivotal verses of Ephesians 2:8–10 declare that our salvation is entirely a gift from God, and that our expression of this gift is to live lives characterized by purposeful work to benefit our neighbors.

WHAT WILL YOU DO RIGHT NOW WITH YOUR TREASURE?

An inconvenient truth among many who claim allegiance to Christ is that we are indeed expected to obey, to follow through with faith in action, and do good for those people in our midst. In the very same treatise as the Parable of the Sheep and the Goats above, Christ also describes the Parable of the Bags of Gold. The connection between these two parables is unmistakable, and the latter is also worthy of reading once again:

> "Again, it will be like a man going on a journey, who called his servants and entrusted his wealth to them. To one he gave five bags of gold, to another two bags, and to another one bag, each according to his ability. Then he went on his journey. The man who had received five bags of gold went at once and put his money to work and gained five bags more. So also, the one with two bags of gold gained two more. But the man who had received one bag went off, dug a hole in the ground and hid his master's money.
>
> "After a long time the master of those servants returned and settled accounts with them. The man who had received five bags of gold brought the other five. 'Master,' he said, 'you entrusted me with five bags of gold. See, I have gained five more.'
>
> "His master replied, 'Well done, good and faithful servant! You have been faithful with a few things; I will put you in charge of many things. Come and share your master's happiness!'
>
> "The man with two bags of gold also came. 'Master,' he said, 'you entrusted me with two bags of gold; see, I have gained two more.'
>
> "His master replied, 'Well done, good and faithful servant! You have been faithful with a few things; I will put you in charge of many things. Come and share your master's happiness!'
>
> "Then the man who had received one bag of gold came. 'Master,' he said, 'I knew that you are a hard man, harvesting where you have not sown and gathering where you have

> not scattered seed. So I was afraid and went out and hid your gold in the ground. See, here is what belongs to you.'
>
> "His master replied, 'You wicked, lazy servant! So you knew that I harvest where I have not sown and gather where I have not scattered seed? Well then, you should have put my money on deposit with the bankers, so that when I returned I would have received it back with interest.
>
> "'So take the bag of gold from him and give it to the one who has ten bags. For whoever has will be given more, and they will have an abundance. Whoever does not have, even what they have will be taken from them. And throw that worthless servant outside, into the darkness, where there will be weeping and gnashing of teeth'" (Matthew 25:14–30).

This preview of our upcoming report to Christ is rich with consequences for both our lives day-by-day and for our spiritual destiny. Stewardship and Responsibility are stressed. The bags of gold represent our resources, abilities, and opportunities. The differing amounts signify how Christ distributes gifts according to each one's capacity. Yet the expectation for all of us remains the same: faithful use of what has been entrusted.

Faithfulness Over Fear is also emphasized. The parable contrasts the faithful initiative of the first two servants with the fearful inaction of the third. The faithful servants understand that the master expects them to work and multiply what they have received, and they act accordingly. The third servant, however, is paralyzed by fear and distrust, resulting in his acts of cowardice.

The Joy of the Master is clearly visible as the faithful servants are rewarded not only with increased trust and responsibilities but also with the invitation to, "Come and share your master's happiness," implying that those who serve Christ faithfully will share in His eternal gladness.

Finally, this parable demonstrates **Judgment and Consequences.** The third servant's inaction is as culpable as outright disobedience and his fate is severe, being cast into outer darkness, separated from Christ. The fate of the third servant emphasizes the seriousness of neglecting to use the treasures entrusted to us all.

WHAT IS INSIDE YOUR BAGS OF GOLD?

The process of discovering your unique skills and genius can be profound and inspiring. Begin by exploring and identifying your spiritual and material gifts. Ask those in your faith community to walk through this experience with you, providing their input about what they observe as your strengths and weaknesses. Engage in serving others, applying what you have discerned to be your spiritual gifts, noting both continued feedback from your peers and the sense of passion you may experience as you proceed. This process may take time, so be patient as you catalog the treasures you possess.

Especially consider the long-term implications of how you use your treasure. Some actions provide immediate benefits, like urgently feeding a hungry person or making a one-time donation to help today's tornado victims. Others have lasting impact, such as developing modern seeds and fertilizers to improve long-term food production or establishing an endowment to support disaster relief for decades. Both types of investments are equally important.

BEGIN INVESTING WITH THE END IN FOCUS

An enlightening exercise — one that may help you apply with excellence the Parable of the Sheep and Goats and Parable of the Bags of Gold — is to compose your own eulogy. That is, to write a statement which summarizes your life in 200–300 words. Such a eulogy would be read at your funeral or posted online with your death announcement. This composition can be a powerful exercise in self-assessment and life planning, culminating in a statement of the legacy you wish to establish. Here is an example of a eulogy template one could use:

________________________ was born in
Your Name
________________________ on ________________________.

As a child, ________________________ was known for
Your Name
____.

________________________ grew up having a close
Your Name
relationship with ________________________.

____________________________ also was passionate about
Your Name

____.

____________________________ especially
Your Name
thought that ______________________ mattered.

____________________________ made a powerful impact
Your Name
on ______________________ and will be remembered for

____.

The most powerful potential outcome of writing your eulogy, however, is not retrospective. Rather, this composition can prompt you to live intentionally today, making choices based upon your trust in Christ that result in ongoing actions of kindness, service, and mercy. Additionally, writing your eulogy helps you to appreciate the time on earth that you still have left, and therefore to prioritize activities that matter most.

OTHERS INSPIRED BY YOUR EXAMPLE

As you proceed to faithfully invest your treasures, it is inevitable that others will note your example and emulate some elements of your life. Alexandra Edwards was an INMED learner in International Medicine and Public Health. For her service-learning element, Alexandra was mentored by Victor Fredlund, a British physician who was going on 40 years of service in southern Africa. She wrote to INMED:

> When I was a medical student, I completed the INMED Graduate Diploma and went on an elective to South Africa in 2011. I was at Mseleni Hospital over Christmas. It was there that I heard the Gospel for the first time, preached by Dr. Fredlund, my attending physician at a Christmas gathering. At that time, I wasn't open to the words, but they started to work on me. The whole experience had a major impact on me, ultimately culminating in my belief in Jesus Christ, becoming a follower, being baptized, and now preparing to embark on a medical mission with my church

> in Zimbabwe. I wanted to thank you for that opportunity and thank Dr. Fredlund.

Beyond his impact on Alexandra at the Christmas gathering, the example of Victor Fredlund is instructive for us all. He was serving humble people far from any limelight and distant from any worldly compensation. Yet perhaps for these very reasons, Dr. Fredlund's confidence in Christ and his message of the Gospel were so powerful within the life of Alexandra.

TREASURES IN HEAVEN

Most all of us enjoy special events: baby showers, birthday parties, New Year's events, Christmas celebrations, sporting competitions. But there is an event approaching more consequential than any other: the day foretold in Matthew 25 when we will give account and each be judged for our use of the Master's treasures. This is the true End Game. This is the actual **Return On Investment.** In this light, Christ implores us:

> "Do not store up for yourselves treasures on earth, where moths and vermin destroy, and where thieves break in and steal. But store up for yourselves treasures in heaven, where moths and vermin do not destroy, and where thieves do not break in and steal. For where your treasure is, there your heart will be also" (Matthew 6:19–21).

This profound command presses us to focus not on temporary riches or worldly success, but rather to prioritize our relationship with Christ and those values that are great in His sight: giving generously to those in need, using our resources to advance His Kingdom, and maintaining an eternal perspective in daily decision-making. This focus also helps us to cultivate a heart that truly values faith and service over possessions or status — demonstrating through our own experience the reality of Christ's words that where your treasure is, there your heart will be also.

The promise of treasures in heaven and the assurance of accountability for our actions, whether good or evil, is powerful motivation for upright living. "How will I explain and justify this action or inaction to Christ?" is a pivotal question to frequently ask regarding our personal behavior as well as the behavior of our companies, businesses, schools, churches, governments, militaries, and institutions of all kinds. We do well to remember how easily influenced and deceived followers of Christ are by the worldly systems that honor strength over mercy and rewards might over right — all the while criticizing as sheer weakness the eternal virtues of humility, justice, and generosity.

JUST DO IT!

Our lives are meant to be characterized by love in action. Christ assures us, "If you love me, keep my commands. … Whoever has my commands and keeps them, is the one who loves me. … Anyone who loves me will obey my teaching. …" (John 14:15, 21, 23). Christ is confirming that genuine love for Him cannot be separated from our outward behavior.

We can distinguish those who love God by the way they live. True agape is love in motion. James, another of Christ's disciples, explains. "Suppose a brother or a sister is without clothes and daily food. If one of you says to them, "Go in peace; keep warm and well fed," but does nothing about their physical needs, what good is it? In the same way, faith by itself, if it is not accompanied by action, is dead."(James 2:15–17). Children are destined to grow. Ships are built to go to sea. Muscles are created to be flexed. Likewise, followers of Christ are new creations purposed to serve humanity.

Action is the final step. Our allegiance to Christ, our mission to love Him and one another, and our specific decisions and plans account for very little unless we put them into practice. And as we act, a wonderful outcome often results: our allegiance to Christ, our sense of mission, our decision making, and our skill at serving others simultaneously improve. Like a positive feedback loop, our confidence and expertise in handling life's opportunities continues to grow and we are even more likely to take action in the future, moving from being simply charitable to becoming extravagantly generous.

COMING FULL CIRCLE BACK IN CHINA

One winter day in 2015, Dr. Jason Pang approached me at LIGHT's H'Image Doctor clinic in the city of Shenyang. "I would like your advice about caring for a difficult diagnosis." His frozen breath was visible with each word in the below-zero temperature air. "In my

INMED Graduate Certificate I learned how to manage common complications of HIV infection, but this patient has me baffled." Dr. Pang proceeded to describe a young man with fatty liver disease — a condition where abnormal lipids cumulate within one's liver leading to serious complications like cirrhosis, heart failure, and even liver cancer.

"Dr. Pang," I replied, "It would be very helpful to examine your patient." Then I added doubtfully, "But maybe your patient would not feel comfortable coming to our hospital complex."

"Ah," returned Jason Pang with an intriguing grin, "I have created a solution!"

An hour later, Dr. Pang and I arrived on location at the Catholic church building. Its ornate Gothic style contrasted sharply with the surrounding cinder block buildings, and within, a population of patients no less dissimilar.

"Christ loves all people, especially those who are HIV-positive," declared Dr. Pang. "So, I approached this church about using their space." His eyes spanned the room, where a dozen men were receiving medical consultations. "Here, we manage their wounds, their diabetes, their sexually transmitted diseases. We wear no masks — they don't protect against HIV anyway — and we have no guards at the door. And since these precious people are largely unemployed, all medical care is provided for free."

Dr. Pang and I together examined his patient with fatty liver disease. The young man appeared gaunt, malnourished. Our treatment plan included control of his diabetes, his hyperlipidemia, and continuance of his critical HIV medication. Jason Pang offered to pray with him, to which the sickened man replied with an affirming smile.

As he prayed, my heart was filled with joy to not only see this outcast man being cared for with compassion, but also to see my colleague, Dr. Pang, so diligently and consistently investing his own treasure toward the well-being of such people.

Concluding his intercession, Jason Pang turned to me. "Nicholas," he declared with all sincerity, "when I care for this man and those like him, I sense my Master's happiness!"

Jason Pang, INMED Graduate and leader of LIGHT – Liaoning International General Heath Trainers, with Nicholas Comninellis, Xi'an, China, 2017. Credit: Author's photo.

AUTHOR'S NOTE

Treasure. We all possess under our control some resources, time, and abilities. Trustworthy use of our treasure has powerful consequences, both to honor Christ and to genuinely benefit of humankind. What's more, our lives intentionally focused on enhancing the welfare of others illuminate the richest life and lifestyle of all.

—Nicholas